FLAMINGOES COMING TO ROOST ON THE FLATS OF A SODA LAKE

GOLIATH HERON BACKED BY PAPYRUS

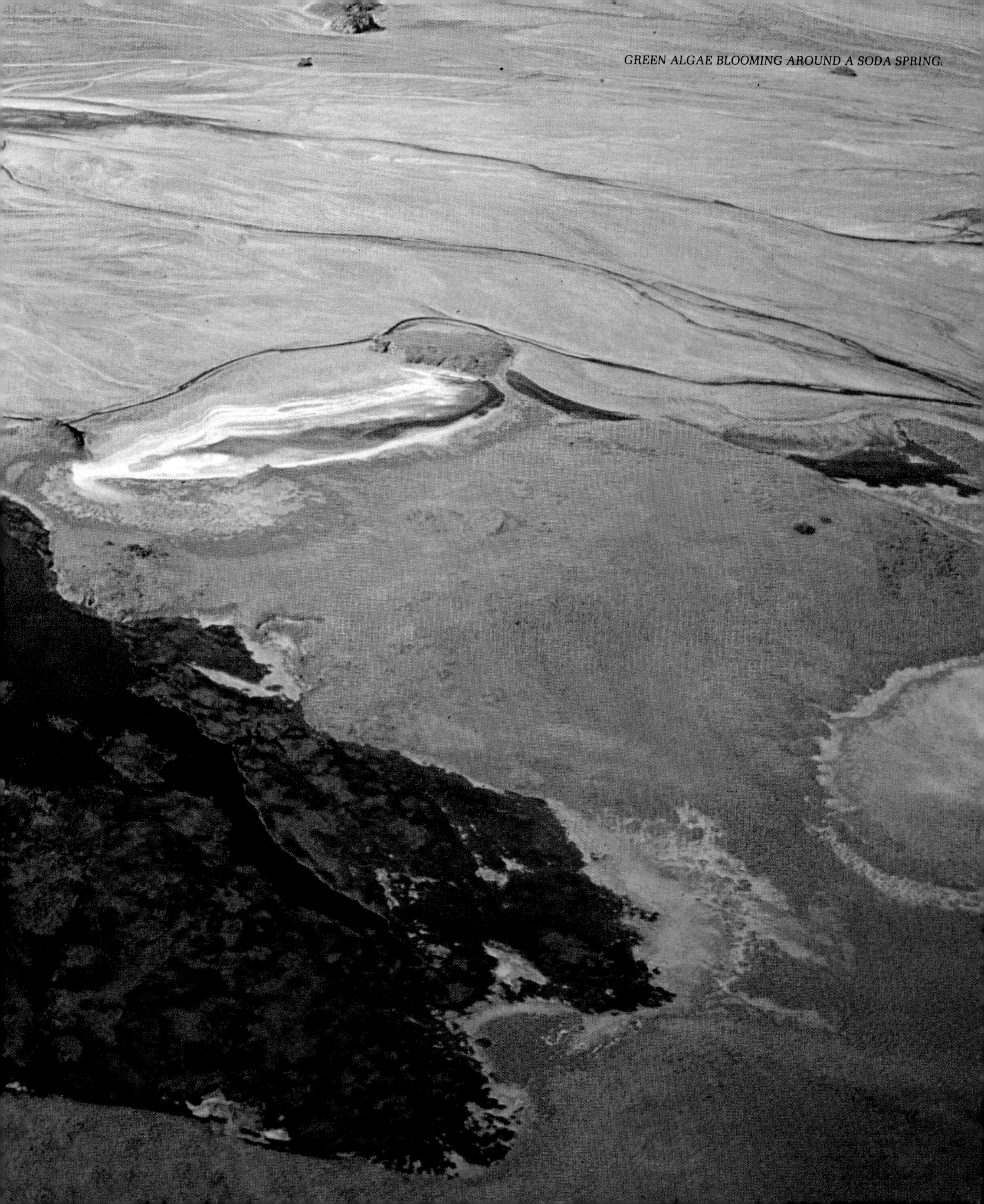

GREEN ALGAE BLOOMING AROUND A SODA SPRING.

THE RIFT'S LARGEST LAKE, RUDOLF, AT DAWN

AFRICA'S RIFT VALLEY

THE WORLD'S WILD PLACES/TIME-LIFE BOOKS/AMSTERDAM

BY COLIN WILLOCK
AND THE EDITORS OF TIME-LIFE BOOKS

WITH PHOTOGRAPHS BY GOETZ D. PLAGE

THE WORLD'S WILD PLACES

Editorial Staff for *Africa's Rift Valley*:
EDITOR: John Man
Deputy Editor: Simon Rigge
Picture Editor: Pamela Marke
Design Consultant: Louis Klein
Staff Writers:
Tony Long, Robert Stewart,
Timberlake Wertenbaker, Heather Wyatt
Picture Researcher: Kerry Arnold
Art Director: Graham Davis
Design Assistant: Joyce Mason
Editorial Co-ordinator: Vanessa Kramer
Editorial Assistant: Jackie Matthews

Consultants
Botany: Phyllis Edwards
Geology: Dr. Peter Stubbs
Ichthyology: Alwyne Wheeler
Invertebrates: Dr. Michael Tweedie
Ornithology: I. J. Ferguson-Lees
Zoology: Dr. P. J. K. Burton

The captions and text of the picture essays are written
by the editorial staff of Time-Life Books.

Published by Time-Life International (Nederland) B.V.
Ottho Heldringstraat 5, Amsterdam 1018.

Colin Willock is an executive director of Survival Anglia Ltd., which specializes in the making of wildlife films. One of Survival's recent films, *The Flight of the Snowgeese*, won two television Emmy awards. Once assistant editor of *Picture Post*, he has written more than 20 books, including *The Enormous Zoo*, a profile of the Uganda national parks. He has travelled extensively in Africa while writing and producing Survival films. Three of his novels, *The Animal Catchers, Coast of Loneliness*, and *Hazanda* are set there.

Dr. W. T. W. Morgan, the consultant for this book, is the author of *East Africa*, a standard geography of the area. He is a graduate of London University and received his doctorate from Northwestern University, Illinois, before becoming Professor of Geography at University College, Nairobi. He later returned to England to teach at King's College, London, and is now lecturing at the University of Durham.

The Cover: Stained grey by its coating of fresh alkaline ash, the active cone of the volcano Ol Doinyo Lengai, the "Mountain of God" of Masai tribesmen, dominates the Rift in Tanzania.

Contents

1/ A Scar on the Earth's Face   16
Signs of Subterranean Turmoil   28
2/ The Danakil Inferno   38
A Landscape of Salt   48
3/ The Fish and the Fish-Eaters   60
A Nature Walk Through Hell's Gate   82
4/ Cauldrons of Soda   96
Caustic Swamps and Bitter Waters   106
5/ Flamingoes by the Million   116
The Flamingoes' Sodary Home   122
6/ People from the Past   132
Into the Dark Continent in 1887   142
7/ The Elephants of Manyara   152
The Moment of Fear   168

Bibliography   180
Acknowledgements and Credits   181
Index   182

A Land under Stress

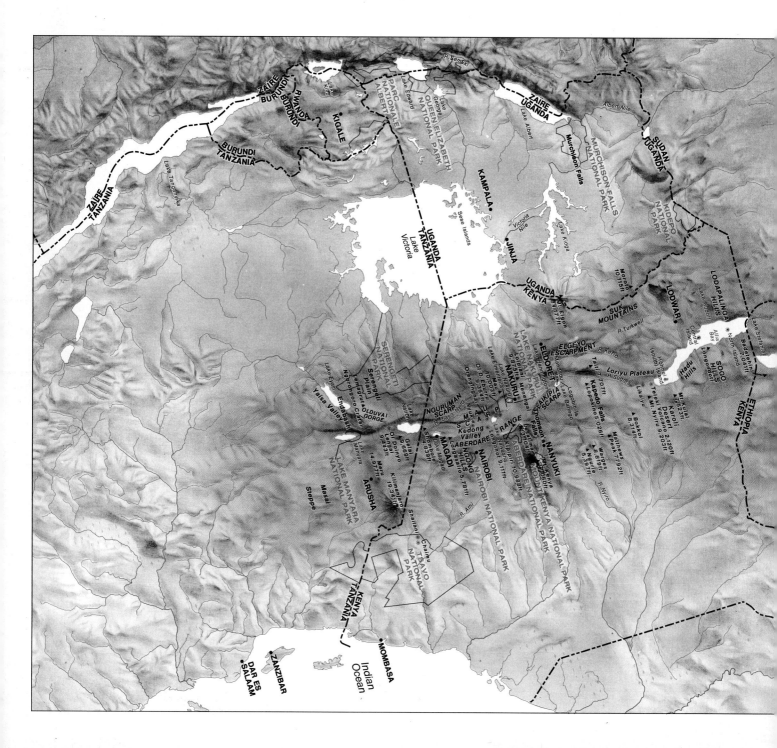

The Great Rift Valley is a 4,000-mile fissure in the earth's crust, stretching from the Lebanon to Mozambique. Its most dramatic section is in the area of East Africa indicated by the brown rectangle on the outline map (right). In the 1,500 miles between the Red Sea and Lake Manyara, a deep subsidence cuts through the continent. It starts with the Y-shaped Danakil Depression and runs south like a pale corridor through the darker high land, continuing in the middle down Lake Rudolf. It was formed by violent subterranean forces that tore apart the earth's crust, causing huge chunks to sink between parallel fault lines and forcing up molten rock in volcanic eruptions. Evidence that rifting is still in progress comes from the 30 active or semi-active volcanoes (red asterisks) and from the boiling springs that bubble up sodium carbonate, turning many lakes along the Great Rift to bitter water or blistering soda flats.

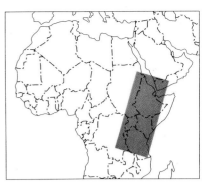

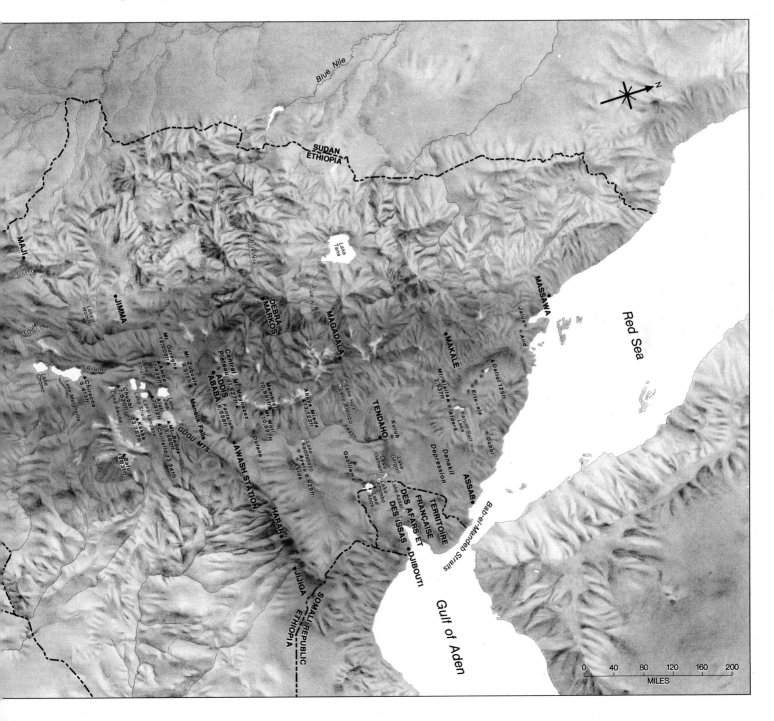

1/ A Scar on the Earth's Face

The natural boundaries of the geographer are rarely described by right lines; wherever these occur the geologist may look for something remarkable. HUGH MILLER/ OLD RED SANDSTONE

I first saw the Great Rift Valley during a journey north from Nairobi, the capital of Kenya. Thirty miles from the city, I came suddenly, without any warning, to the lip of a gigantic chasm. The scrub-covered slope fell away almost vertically in front of me. Spread out 2,000 feet below was an immense yellow plain, stretching into the distance. Thirty miles away, blue in the haze, I could see another almost vertical wall, very similar to the one on which I stood, rising to the same height. The whole landscape was so regular, so continuous, that it appeared almost unnatural. On either side of me, the valley wall stretched north and south in a straight line as far as the eye could see—and the distant wall did the same. There are very few straight lines, let alone parallel straight lines, in nature. Yet, as anyone looking down into the chasm would realize, only the most powerful forces of nature could have created a trench so colossal in scale.

The cliff-like walls of the valley appeared fresh and comparatively unweathered. I was unable to resist the impression that they had been formed not long ago, and that the entire valley floor had subsided from the level of the plateau in one enormous piece, like a lift 30 miles across going down a gigantic lift shaft. This is approximately what happened, not just here, but over thousands of miles to north and south. Over the last 20 million years—very recently in geological time—global disturbances tore at the continental masses of the Middle East and Africa and created a great scar down one-sixth of the earth's circumference. The part of the Great Rift Valley I first saw is a particularly dramatic point on a 4,000-mile line of subsidences between the Lebanon in the north and Mozambique in the south. From the Jordan valley, the scar runs through the ocean-filled trench of the Red Sea until it touches Africa in the low-lying Danakil desert of northern Ethiopia. From here it continues as a huge trench, rarely more than 30 miles wide, climbing and plunging through the landscape of East Africa. First it rises steeply into the Ethiopian highlands and travels south at 6,000 feet above sea level, its journey signposted by a series of lakes, the walls of the valley broken by cross fractures. Then down into Kenya, through Lake Rudolf, rising to Lake Naivasha, the highest lake in the valley, then on past the point where I had stood, through more lakes and down again into Tanzania and Mozambique until it finally peters out beyond Lake Nyasa, heading towards the Indian Ocean.

From this great crack in the earth's crust, there are other, lesser cracks that branch off: the Gulf of Suez and Gulf of Aqaba stretch out from the northern end of the Red Sea, and the Gulf of Aden from its southern end; in Africa, a lesser, western rift, containing, among others, Lakes Albert and Tanganyika, curves northwards from Lake Nyasa like the branch of a plant growing up from one side of the stem, in this case the main trunk of the Rift.

Geologists believe that some of the most recent major happenings in the formation of this great rift system took place within the last 10,000 years. Certainly there is a wealth of associated stories and legends to lend credence to the occurrence of cataclysmic earth movements within the time span of man's accumulated memory.

The Somalis, referring perhaps to a time before some major rifting occurred, claim that their ancestors travelled from Arabia to Africa over dry land, across the present straits of Bab-el-Mandeb, at the southern end of the Red Sea. The Old Testament, picking up the story, tells how the Egyptians, in pursuit of the Israelites, were caught and engulfed by the Red Sea: possibly a local arm of the sea was then in the process of formation. The Old Testament also describes an event which may have occurred at the same time, when the biblical cities of Sodom and Gomorrah, now thought by archaeologists to have been situated just south of the Dead Sea, in the line of the Rift, were destroyed by "fire and brimstone". The natives of Ujiji—where the explorer Livingstone made his base before his discovery of Lake Nyasa in 1859—tell long-ago stories about the African part of the Rift, where a great flood is said to have inundated plains rich in game and cattle, so forming Lake Tanganyika.

None of this literally earth-shattering past was investigated or even suspected by Europeans until the late 19th Century, when attention began to focus on the main trunk of the Great Rift Valley in Kenya, where my own travels were to be concentrated. Their ignorance was not surprising, for the colonial powers had barely penetrated inland from the coasts. Although Arab caravans trading in slaves and ivory had crossed the Rift on their journeys from Mombasa, on the coast, to Uganda for hundreds of years, there were no maps to be had. The first maps were not even made until the 1860s, when two amateur cartographers, T. Wakefield and Clemens Denhardt of Mombasa, drew a series based on lengthy questioning of the Arab traders. Considering they were drawn from hearsay, these maps were remarkably full and accurate, but they naturally had some notable failings. They were very poor on the location of rivers and lakes, and particularly on the actual sizes. They vastly exaggerated the extent of Lake Baringo and left out Lake Hannington. Above all, they failed to mention or depict the line of the Great Rift Valley at all.

If the map-makers were still making guesses, the geologists had not even started work—nor could they until there was more for them to go on. But now the time of the explorers had arrived. In the 1880s, a pioneering group of travellers revealed the mysteries of the East African Rift, the most pronounced section of the whole system. Although they did not draw wide conclusions from their piecemeal discoveries, they rapidly provided the missing parts of the puzzle. In 1883, the German naturalist, Dr. Gustav Fischer, became the first man to enter Masailand, as the territory of the warlike Masai tribesmen was then commonly known. He described the country stretching from the volcano, Ol Doinyo Lengai, in the south, in what is now Tanzania, to a spot just north of Lake Naivasha in Kenya, where he ran out of supplies. He had explored the line of the Great Rift Valley just beyond the point where I had first seen it. Later the same year, the Scottish explorer, Joseph Thomson, pushed further north, passing beyond Lake Naivasha where the Masai were now at their most bellicose, until he reached Lake Baringo. He was able to reveal that, far from being the enormous expanse of water shown on Wakefield and Denhardt's map of the 1860s, Baringo was barely five miles wide by 14 miles long. Meanwhile, the German explorer, Baumann, had provided details about the area around Lake Manyara in the south, beyond which point the walls of the Rift cease to be so clearly defined and the line of the valley becomes diffuse.

The discoverer of the Great Rift Valley, J. W. Gregory, remarked long before the space age that the Rift would be one earth feature visible from the moon. His prediction is borne out by this picture, taken from Apollo 17 at a distance of 90,000 miles, showing all of Africa, with the Mediterranean at the very top and the Arabian peninsula near the top. Just below the southern tip of Arabia can be seen the Y of the northern end of the Rift, enclosing the light patch of the Danakil Depression. Clouds obscure much of the valley to the south.

In 1887 came the most important discovery of all. The Hungarian sportsman Count Teleki and his gifted companion, a German artist, Ludwig von Höhnel, marched 300 miles from the coast to discover the vast lake which was still a traders' tale for Europeans. It was then called by its African name, Basso Narok. Having discovered what the African tribesmen had known was there all the time—this to me is the perpetual irony of the white man's exploration of Africa—he renamed Basso Narok "Rudolf" after the Austrian crown prince, who was his sponsor. Its smaller, marshy and even more remote companion to the north-east, Basso Ebor, he called Lake Stefanie, after Prince Rudolf's consort.

The knowledge of the size and position of these lakes, especially Lake Rudolf, the most northerly of the new "discoveries", was immensely important. Plotted on the map, they appeared as links in a connected chain leading north to the Red Sea. The first significant deduction from this new information was made in 1891 by the Viennese geologist, Eduard Suess, who had never been to Africa, but had collected the explorers' accounts on his desk. He declared that the whole line of country from Lake Nyasa in the south to the river Jordan in the north had been fractured by a connected series of earth movements. He used the contemporary geologists' term to describe the phenomenon. He called it a *Graben*, or grave. However, there was one key figure yet to come upon the scene who would explore the valley scientifically, diagnose it for what it was, and bring it to world attention. That figure was another Scot, the young geologist John Walter Gregory.

Gregory was the son of a Scottish wool merchant trading in Bermondsey, south London. He was trained to be a merchant too, but as a colleague later put it, "an overmastering bent for natural history rescued him from business and secured him for science". After studying at London University, he was appointed in 1887, at the age of 23, to the geological department of the British Museum of Natural History in Kensington. Gregory was an ardent follower of Suess and agreed with him that there was once a super-continent, Gondwanaland, which broke up to form the present southern continents. The movements that pulled the continents apart, he believed, were also responsible for tearing at the fabric of Africa and causing the subsidence of the Rift. However, it was still a theory, developed from the observations of explorers who were not experts, and Gregory now felt he must see the Rift for himself and discover empirical support for his beliefs.

In 1892 Gregory got his chance. He was asked to go as naturalist on an expedition across Somalia, and accepted the invitation with enthusiasm. Unfortunately the journey was a disaster. Bad planning, bad Somali porters and lack of food forced the party to turn back from the interior after only six weeks, and Gregory ended up in the port of Mombasa, far to the south, with malaria, dysentery and an unshakeable determination to mount his own expedition. He decided to follow the ancient Arab caravan route inland from Mombasa. Despite repeated discouragement from Europeans, who urged him not to venture into the little known territory of the hostile Kikuyu and Masai tribes, Gregory left Mombasa on March 23, 1893, at the head of 40 men. He was accompanied for a little while by two European officials, who gaily sent the balding, lanky Scotsman off with the refrain of "Will he nae come back again?" Gregory, suffering from another bout of malaria, wondered wistfully whether he would.

In order to diagnose Suess's *Graben* geologically, Gregory intended to adopt the geologists' standard method of discovery and make a "section" right across the valley, collecting rock samples from selected points and using them to draw a cross-section diagram of the rock strata underlying both the walls and the floor. He knew that, if he chose a suitable spot to make the section and was successful in collecting his samples, the resulting diagram would enable him to prove to the world how the Rift had actually come about. Nothing is simple for the field geologist. Assuming that the valley floor had been created by a gigantic subsidence, Gregory expected to find the picture complicated by the other events which would surely have occurred during the immense time span of a geological happening. Lava streaming in from the volcanic eruptions along the fault lines at the edges as the floor sank down would have covered much of the valley floor; immense deposits of silt would have been laid down by the lakes that have filled much of the valley with water at varying times and at varying levels; different parts of the valley may have slipped to different positions. The end result of so complex a pattern of events is an intricate layering and apparent confusion of rocks which initially defies sense.

The first spot Gregory chose for his section was near Lake Naivasha, and he spent five weeks marching through Kikuyu and Masai country to reach it. On the journey, he revealed a remarkable talent for diplomacy, knowing when to yield to native intransigence and when to show toughness. When he arrived at the Rift, however, seeing it initially at a point close to my own first glimpse, he found that the area round Naivasha was a hotspot of Masai belligerence. The tribesmen were not only busy slaughtering Kikuyu but also harassing and even attacking any caravan or traveller who seemed insufficiently protected. Diplomacy was little use here, and Gregory was forced to move another hundred miles to the north where he reached Lake Baringo, an extremely lucky accident both for him and future geologists.

The cross-section of the valley at Lake Baringo is one of the most spectacular of all. In the east, where Gregory had arrived, the wall of the Laikipia escarpment, 7,000 feet above sea level, drops down towards the lake, ending in a series of step-like foothills. Then, ten miles from the foot of the escarpment, comes the lake with its green islands and beyond, another ten miles to the west, what at first looks like the other wall of the valley. In fact, this is a great block called Kamasia, or the Tugen Hills after the Tugen tribe which lives there. Only after climbing its crest to an altitude of 7,000 feet can one see that a further ten miles to the west, beyond the valley of the river Kerio, rises one of the most imposing escarpments of all, the Elgeyo scarp, also 7,000 feet high. Elgeyo, not Kamasia, is the western wall of the valley.

This confusion right across the valley was a godsend for Gregory, since it enabled him more easily to discover the nature of the underlying strata. Perhaps his opportunity can best be understood by picturing the countryside before the great subsidence took place. It was then level land from the plains on top of Laikipia to the plateau on top of Elgeyo, in the west. Now think of it, not as a slice of Africa, but as a broad, multi-decker sandwich. Bread, butter and fillings represent different strata composed of lavas, sediments and the hard crystalline rocks of the continent. At first, only the smooth top layer of bread is visible. Then the sandwich is cut into six segments—two large ones at the edges and four thin strips in the middle—by parallel, north-south lines. This represents the tearing and cracking of Africa. The large segment on the right stays where it is—the Laikipia plains—but the next slips down a little, splitting into smaller sections that each slip down a little more— the foothills. The third slides down a great deal further and receives some extra layers of bread and fillings on top. This represents Lake Baringo and its shoreline: the extra layers are the sediments washed into the ancient lake and deposited over the whole of its once great area. The fourth pile is the most important of all: the great block of Kamasia. Instead of sinking, it has tilted violently to the west, revealing the layers of which it consists, including the basic crystalline rocks—gneiss and schists—at the bottom. Beyond Kamasia there is a further fully subsided segment—the valley of the river Kerio—and then, finally, comes

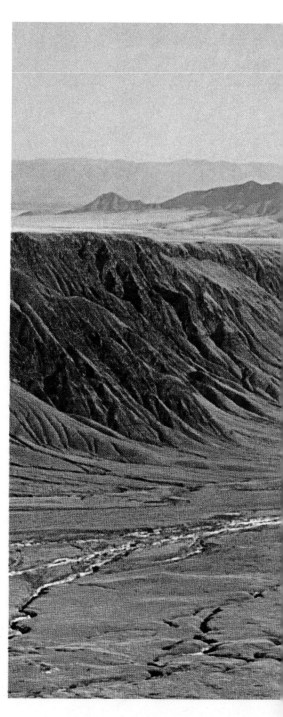

The western Rift wall, opposite Mount Lengai, towers to 1,500 feet, testimony to the great subsidence that created the plain below.

the large, stable segment on the left representing the Elgeyo plateau.

One can imagine Gregory scrambling along the precipitous wall of Laikipia with his geologist's hammer, chipping away in a state of high scientific excitement at the strata exposed when the segment of the foothills slipped. He made his base in the village of Njemps at the south-eastern end of Lake Baringo and set out on a series of rock-gathering excursions around the lake, taking samples of lavas and sediments all the way down, carefully noting where he had found the specimens and at what height. Finally, he climbed the base of the tilted mountain block of Kamasia, storing the vital information about its upturned strata. At this point he ran out of supplies and received warnings of new tribal hostilities nearby. He was forced to abandon his wall-to-wall survey before even studying the Elgeyo scarp. After traversing only half the valley, he returned to Mombasa and sailed for England.

But the expedition had not been a failure. Gregory's feat was to reach the correct conclusions without the missing data. His section of the Baringo basin, pieced together from his own information and from maps, showed the position of the strata that composed the valley floor and its walls. It demonstrated that the layers along the eastern escarp-ment of Laikipia closely matched those in the central block of Kamasia and in Elgeyo, the western escarpment. It portrayed the same layers in the valley floor, but as much as 6,000 feet lower.

Addressing himself to the orthodox geologists of his day, Gregory concluded triumphantly that "these valleys were not formed by removal grain by grain, by rivers or wind, of the rocks which originally occupied them, but by the rock sinking in mass, while the adjacent land remained stationary". Gregory now invented a new term in geology and gave the whole vast feature he had discovered a name to be remembered by. "For this type of valley I suggest the name of Rift Valley, using the term rift in the sense of a relatively narrow space due to subsidence between parallel fractures. Such valleys", he continued, "are known in many parts of the world, but that of East Africa may justly be called the Great Rift Valley".

Gregory wrote two books on his adventures and geological dis-coveries in Africa, and became Professor of Geology at Glasgow University. He subsequently travelled to the Arctic, India and finally South America where he was killed in 1932, at the age of 68, when his canoe capsized in a Peruvian river. Though little known outside his own field, Gregory nevertheless has his memorial: the Great Rift Valley itself. Even today there are a good many people, both geologists and

John Walter Gregory, who was the first geologist to explore the Great Rift Valley, led his own expedition to Lakes Naivasha and Baringo in 1893. His men nicknamed him "bulging pockets" because of his habit of stuffing his pockets with numerous rock samples.

laymen, who still refer to its main trunk simply as the Gregory Rift.

Had he been able to stay in Africa longer and travel to Elgeyo, Gregory would probably have unravelled more than he did. He did not entirely appreciate the amount of in-filling by lavas and sediments on the valley floor—sometimes as deep as a mile. Modern geologists have since discovered it is in the tilt block of Kamasia that the total geological history of the Rift Valley lies revealed, from the lavas and sediments on top down to bedrock at the bottom.

Since Gregory's day, geologists have gradually been building on his work, dating the various stages of the Rift's creation and fitting them into a global picture of earth movements. According to the latest geo-physical conclusions, based on the dating of rocks along the whole of the rift system, rifting took place in three main phases: Triassic (200 million years ago), Cretaceous (between 80 and 130 million years ago) and, finally, Late Cainozoic (the last 20 million years), the period when the eastern Rift was formed. These dates coincide with the chronology of continental drift, the theory which was in its infancy in Gregory's day. In the earliest of the three phases, 200 million years ago, the great super-continent of Gondwanaland, in which Gregory believed so ardently, is considered to have been still in existence. Deep down within the earth, radioactively generated heat produced slow but immensely powerful currents beneath the surface crust, causing the solid rock of the earth's mantle to move like a heavy liquid. As the great subterranean currents rose towards the surface, they came into contact with the crust of the super-continent, where they turned outwards, wrenching Gondwanaland apart. Molten rock spewed up through the cracks as lava in volcanic eruptions and the fragments were slowly carried away to their locations as the present continents. Oceans filled the gaps.

One of these new sea areas is the Indian Ocean, and Madagascar is a piece of Africa that was torn off and carried away. Geologists today sometimes speak of the Great Rift Valley as "an aborted ocean". There, but for the grace of unfathomable underground forces, they say, should have gone a large piece of Africa east of the Rift, floating off like Madagascar. If this had happened, salt water would have filled the Rift until it resembled the Red Sea. The eastern half of Ethiopia, all of Somalia, and half of Kenya and Tanzania would have become a large offshore island. In the event a new sea was not formed.

What did happen was that during the creation of the Indian Ocean there was a great outpouring of molten rock. Much of this material must have come from beneath East Africa, parts of which subsided as a result. The creation of the Great Rift Valley began. In the Oligocene, roughly 40 million years ago, major riftings produced some of the great lakes, the forerunners of today's smaller lakes. Eleven million years ago came the main faulting, followed in the last three million years by subsidiary faulting on the valley floor and the renewal of movements in the main fractures. A bare million years ago the valley's shoulders were uplifted and yet more faulting took place on its floor. All these movements produced intense volcanic activity, as the subsidence of the floor caused the molten rock beneath to be squeezed up at the sides. This volcanic activity goes on today and is evidence of the continuing operation of continental drift. Indeed, the Red Sea and the Gulf of Aden are gradually widening and there is every reason to think that East Africa is now being torn apart and that the Great Rift Valley may well in some tens of millions of years become an ocean after all.

The feeling of a landscape on the move, constantly rearranging itself according to some unfathomable plan, is always strong in the Great Rift Valley. Unlike the plateaux either side of its precipitous walls, which mostly consist of shield rock as much as 3,000 million years old, eroded to a flat monotony, the interior of the valley is a young land. Volcanoes both active and dormant rise at intervals along its length, while steam vents and boiling springs bear added witness to the turmoil beneath. The ground is covered in volcanic ash rich in sodium carbonate, or washing soda, and this has found its way into the lakes, turning many of them bitter or transforming a few into almost solid deposits of soda. Many animals are unable to cope with such extreme conditions, but there is one notable exception: flamingoes thrive on the wealth of diatoms, blue-green algae, found in soda lakes and the millions that live in the Rift provide one of the finest wildlife spectacles to be seen anywhere.

Despite their bitterness, many of the other lakes support a large indigenous population of birds. Thousands of pelicans, egrets, herons, storks, wildfowl and cormorants, as well as kingfishers and fish eagles, can be seen here. The lakes also form staging points along one of the world's most heavily travelled bird migration routes. In early spring, small, familiar birds like swallows and wheatears fly in thousands between the towering walls of the Rift, travelling north to Eastern Europe or Russia. They are joined by storks, cranes, eagles and hawks. Many of these birds are helped on their way by the numerous thermals, currents of hot air that rise up the steep escarpments of the Rift.

The plains of the valley contain some of the last big game herds, including, at Lake Manyara in Tanzania, the highest concentration of elephants per square mile left in Africa. And, distributed throughout the valley, there is a rich variety of wild people, a fair cross-section through the patchwork of African tribes. As anyone who wishes to understand Africa must realize, tribes dictate the realities of territory, emnity and allegiance more often than the lines arbitrarily placed on the map by former colonists. In the extreme north, in the Afar triangle of Ethiopia, live the most savage people I have come across in Africa or anywhere else. The Danakil, a Muslim race possibly descended from the ancient Egyptians, are still liable to murder and castrate strangers to protect their desert home and its scanty water supplies. In the extreme south of the area covered by my travels around Lake Natron, live the tribe who most easily capture the European traveller's imagination, the ochre-daubed Masai who once harassed the explorers. Between these extremes of north and south lie the tribal lands of the adaptable Kikuyu; the Njemps, a fishing tribe close in blood to the Masai; Tugen, Samburu, Pokot, Rendille, Turkana and Galla. Each have a different tradition, language and background. Some grow subsistence crops, some specialize in hunting. Most are herders of cattle, camels or goats.

No one can fail to be impressed by the scenic contrasts of the magnificent country the tribesmen live in. In the Danakil desert in northern Ethiopia, the Rift plunges to a torrid 400 feet below sea level and the temperature soars to the infernal, while along many of its escarpments there are dense and gloomy rain forests, fed by the clouds that often cloak them. And at Naivasha, the highest of the lakes, there is often frost on the morning grass. All this richness and diversity can be found in the most pronounced section of the valley, between the Danakil in the north and Manyara in the south. That is why, in my travels, I concentrated on this 1,500 mile section. I knew that here I would find the wildest and richest scenes to be experienced in the Great Rift Valley of Africa.

Signs of Subterranean Turmoil

The Great Rift Valley is one of the most spectacular volcanic regions in the world, and also one of the least known. Most of its volcanoes are long dead and their gigantic remains now litter its course, geological corpses dominating the land that created them.

But 30 still show some signs of activity. They are the signals that deep down inside the earth, continent-splitting forces are at work along the line of the Rift. Internal heat creates titanic currents which over the ages stir solid rock like stiff treacle. These currents push up and turn outwards beneath the earth's crust, stretching it like opposing conveyor belts. In the process a layer of molten rock, or magma, is built up. When the stretching reaches an intolerable pitch, the earth's crust fractures and magma rushes through, emerging as the molten lava of an erupting volcano.

The classically symmetrical cones of the volcanoes have been built up over millennia of geological activity by the alternation of two kinds of eruption, explosive and effusive. In an explosive eruption, there is a large amount of gas in the magma, which blasts through a chimney-like vent and showers a storm of rocks, ash and molten lava around in a circle. In an effusive eruption, the magma contains less gas and flows out quietly like hot plasticine, covering the previous layer of rock and ash with a coat of lava.

Both types of eruption occurred in the Rift in the 1960s. In the Danakil desert at the northern end of the valley, there was an unusual type of effusive eruption in 1960 that filled the crater at the top of the volcano Erta-ale with molten lava, forming one of the world's rare lava lakes. Then in 1966 there was an explosive eruption in the southern part of the Rift when Ol Doinyo Lengai (opposite) blew up. Because the volcano stands in remote, inhospitable country at the southern end of Lake Natron, an arid soda lake, few people saw the eruption and no world-wide publicity attended the event. However, the roving photographer, Gerald Cubitt, climbed to the lip of the crater twice during the month of the eruption, and took the photographs on this and the next four pages. They show Lengai before, during and after the eruption, from both inside and outside the crater, providing a rare documentation of the changes an eruption brings.

Ol Doinyo Lengai, the Masai "Mountain of God", pours out lava rich in alkali during its 1966 eruption. This type of lava is black when it emerges, but is chemically unstable. Within 48 hours of coating the slopes of the 2,000-foot cone, the lava turns white, for contact with moisture in the air converts much of it to crystals of sodium carbonate—commonly known as washing soda.

Lengai's crater (above), a weird landscape
of congealed white lava, simmers
ominously only a week before its 1966
eruption. The photographer, Gerald
Cubitt, recalled later how he saw "lava
cones gurgitating blobs of molten black
lava, while the ground shook with
rumbles that foretold the coming storm".

On the right, Lengai is seen erupting
only a week after Cubitt had left. He
returned hurriedly to watch the black
cloud billowing 25,000 feet into the air,
raining ash over the mountain. After
three weeks the volcano subsided,
leaving the slopes a chiarascuro of
white ridges and black depressions.

A soft mantle of green covers the outside of Mount Lengai, put on in the quiescent years before the violent explosion of 1966.

A fresh coat of caustic white ash applied during the 1966 explosion gives Lengai's sides and foothills a wintry appearance.

The Distinctive Craters

Perhaps the most striking remnant of a volcanic eruption is the crater as it appears soon after an eruption. Its original shape reveals the type of action that formed it. In an explosive eruption, like those that have wracked many volcanoes in the Danakil, escaping gases leave behind a gaping, often steaming, chimney (opposite). An effusive eruption, on the other hand, wells up inside a dishlike, neatly circular crater.

Typical of the appearance of a volcano following an effusive eruption is Erta-ale, the most spectacular of a chain of five volcanoes that appear etched in statuesque relief against the desert's flat salt plains. Erta-ale's present crater (right) was formed in 1960 by an effusive eruption witnessed by Paul Mohr, a geologist in Ethiopia. He saw a lava lake of red hot, pasty basalt fill the volcano's crater, gushing out of fissures in its sides. From this scene of elemental alchemy billowed a cloud of steam, giving renewed justification to the name Erta-ale, which in the language of the Danakil tribesmen means "fuming mountain".

A lake of white lava wells up in Erta-ale's crater during the effusive eruption of 1960.

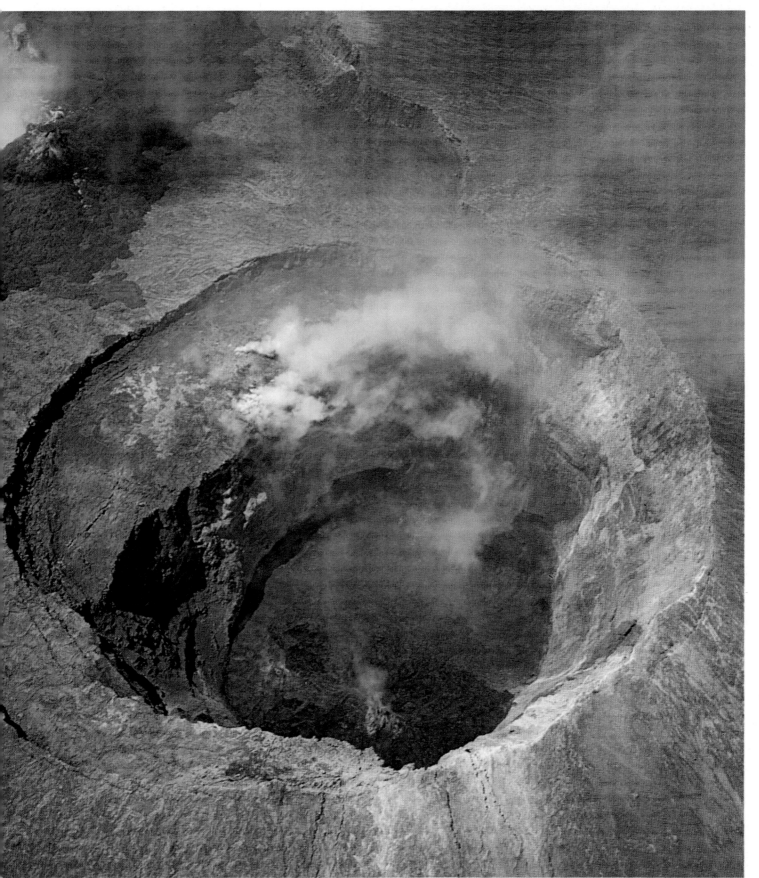

The crater of a Danakil volcano emits steam, the main source of the explosion that blasted it open, causing its chimney-like appearance.

Aftermath of an Explosion

Soon after the eruption, a volcano loses the top of its neat cone and remains disfigured until a shroud of vegetation cloaks it in old age. The change comes about when the top of the cone collapses, falling into the space left in the volcano's substructure by the movements of rock or magma during the eruption. The collapse of the cone gives the volcano a decapitated look from the outside and determines the form of the depression inside the summit.

Known normally as a crater but, if very large, as a caldera, this depression is always many times the diameter of the original vent. The most impressive of such calderas in the Rift Valley belong to two large old volcanoes rising between lakes Baringo and Magadi. The more northerly volcano, Menengai, has a caldera shaped like a shallow soup plate, seven miles wide, with titanic chips in its rim and a jumble of immense boulders on its floor. The southerly volcano, Suswa, has an outer caldera of five miles and an inner one of three miles. This contains a lava island which at its last eruption was cut off from the sides by a molten moat.

Between these two calderas lies Longonot, whose eruption long ago caused a different but equally dramatic type of collapse: deep rather than wide. The crater is only one mile wide, but it has steep sides and bores into the earth like a gigantic cannon barrel, seeming barely to await the touch of subterranean heat before firing.

Small patches of scrub grow in the pit of an extinct crater on the shore of Lake Rudolf.

The senile volcano, Longonot, breathes steam through the foliage on its crater, just as it has done for a century without exploding.

2/ The Danakil Inferno

Dregs of water . . . were measured out among us, in Danakil, as
though they had been the contents of the last bottle
of some priceless vintage wine.   L. M. NESBITT/ DESERT AND FOREST

The hottest, lowest, most inhospitable section of the African Rift lies in the far north, separated from the Red Sea only by a range of low hills. It is the scorching Ethiopian desert, the Danakil, the lowest part of which is called, in the more precise language of geographers and geologists, the Danakil Depression. Depression is an apt word, since much of the Danakil lies 400 feet below sea level, forming a great hollow of 58,000 square miles in the earth's surface. Deep down in the Depression, the surface temperature of the rock can rise to an incredible 320 degrees Fahrenheit—more than hot enough to fry a chicken.

The Danakil, sometimes known as the Afar triangle after the Afar tribesmen who are virtually its only inhabitants, is, in fact, shaped like a south-pointing equilateral triangle. Its base stretches along the Red Sea between the sea-port of Massawa in the west and Ethiopia's border with the old French Somaliland, now known as Territoire Française des Afars et des Issas, in the east. Its apex is wedged tightly into the great Ethiopian highlands where the river Awash has cut a deep gorge as it tumbles to lose itself in the desert inferno. Just west of the gorge, 8,000 feet above sea level, stands the capital, Addis Ababa. At this point the Danakil ends and the Rift narrows to a trench about 30 miles wide, in which form it continues more or less unbroken for 1,000 miles southwards to Lake Manyara in Tanzania. Almost precisely at the centre of the Danakil is Tendaho, a small settlement with an air-strip.

It was from here that I flew by helicopter to explore the triangular desert.

The landscape looks either like the end of the world, or its beginning. I have never viewed the aftermath of an atomic explosion at close quarters, but the Danakil might well be the kind of landscape such an explosion produces. The colours are those of desert and of volcanic fire: greys, whites and yellows intermingled with ochres, deep browns and ember reds. Mud-coloured buttresses and miniature mesas lie jumbled together. Glistening salt plains stretch towards towering pinnacles, also encrusted with salt. Deep green pits appear to boil and bubble. Volcanoes belch smoke or leave grey scars where the lava of centuries has cooled. Nothing but the hardiest of plants, animals and birds can survive here.

The only exception to this barren landscape is the ribbon of green fed by the river Awash as it winds its way north-eastwards across the southern part of the Danakil. The river provides the sole support for the Danakil's 200,000 nomadic Afar herdsmen. They believe that "he who controls the water controls the Danakil", and any intruders who might threaten their lonely tenure are murdered and castrated, not necessarily in that order.

The weird, primeval appearance of the Danakil stems mainly from the fact that it is still an area of intense geological activity, as its volcanoes bear witness. It is being subjected to the continent-tearing forces, not only of the African Rift of which it is part, but also of two other adjacent arms of the rift systems: the Red Sea and the Gulf of Aden. Consequently it is prone to severe earthquakes. From May to September, 1961, for example, several shocks were recorded measuring 6.5 on the Richter scale, which has a maximum of ten.

Over millions of years, this type of activity gradually created the Depression as it appears today, probably by making its central area slip down between parallel faults to form a trench. In very recent times, possibly only 10,000 years ago, part of the Danakil was under water, and extended south as an arm of the Red Sea. Later, however, the crust rose, setting up the line of hills along the base of the triangle and cutting off the Danakil sea, leaving its waters to evaporate and form the great salt plains of the present Depression.

The old fault lines are now partly obscured, but their presence is marked by the line of the Danakil volcanoes, both active and dormant, and by lurid-coloured hot springs. These, too, are a sign of volcanic activity. When surface water seeps down through the fault cracks, it comes into contact with molten rock beneath and is then forced upwards through layers of salts and minerals, emerging boiling hot and coloured according to the type of mineral compound it has passed through. Brown, yellow and red, for instance, are colours picked up from the various ox-ides and hydroxides of iron. As the water cools, its minerals crystallize and form coloured stalagmites, humps and mounds. Many of the salts laid down in the process provide colour in a more indirect way, forming a specialized environment for many brightly-hued species of algae.

The Danakil's geological history is still vague because its inhospitality has kept out explorers. Apart from the Afar, very few others—mainly European and American miners and researchers—have ever walked on it. One Swiss and two Italian expeditions made ill-fated forays into it in the 19th Century. They travelled the shortest route, east-west across the desert, but it proved to be extremely arduous and they either died of thirst and starvation or were massacred.

It was not until 1928 that an Englishman, L. M. Nesbitt, and two Italians, T. Pastori and G. Rosina, managed to cross the north-western part of the Danakil the long way, 800 miles from Addis Ababa to the Red Sea. Their march took three and a half months, and three Ethiopian companions, three mules and ten camels died; the rest of the 20-strong party survived, partly as a result, Nesbitt maintained, of "my habit of placing my trust in Providence".

"We started again at daybreak," he wrote in the early stages of his journey, "and soon came to ground covered with tall horny grass which appeared to be entirely dried up and parched. Yet it was not dry within. The desert colours this grass with its own ochre hue, as it colours every-thing else in the dismal landscape. . . . The jet-black mountains to the west were outlined by a thin rim of light, which appeared to separate them from the sky. Presently this gradually went out, and everything became merged in a single, blue-black void, engulfing the earth and sky. Only the stars hung from base to summit of the infinite vault before us."

In 1933 and 1934, one of the great English explorers of the 20th Century, Wilfred Thesiger, first traced the course of the Awash. The river rises in the highlands south of Addis Ababa. For centuries Ethiopians and Europeans alike had assumed that it flowed to an unknown outlet in or near the Red Sea, but no one had ever found its mouth. The disappearance of its mouth, Thesiger said, "has excited considerable curiosity, and many have been the theories expounded to account for the river's failure to reach the sea".

Thesiger set out from Awash Station to map the river on December 1, 1933, "somewhat hurriedly", thinking that the Abyssinian government would forbid his departure for fear of his safety. He had a caravan of

Clouds of Danakil dust swirl around a tribal hut of mats tied over a stick frame, almost obscuring the Ethiopian humped cattle behind.

18 camels, 23 men armed with 13 rifles and an official escort of another 15 armed men. For nearly six months he struggled through "country as dead as a lunar landscape", broken only rarely by oases of green. "Throughout the hottest hours," he wrote, "we crouched among the rocks, our heads swathed in cloths, wondering if we should have the strength left to continue, but nothing could shelter us from the scorching wind which drove before it a stinging cloud of sand."

Thesiger was less afraid than challenged by the Afar tribesmen's "well-merited reputation for savagery". Although he was met once, at Berifer, 70 miles north-west of Awash Station, by "a large gathering of armed warriors" who were "far from friendly", he escaped unharmed. He attempted to investigate the Afar custom of murdering intruders, and to understand it. His report to the Royal Geographical Society in London on November 12, 1934, was packed with details of their culture, carefully studied and for the most part meticulously set down. He did find it difficult, however, to speak "unblushingly" of castration. He generally called the cut testicles "trophies". An Afar's standing in the tribe, he wrote, "depends on the number of his trophies, and ten will give the right to wear a coveted iron bracelet". Nesbitt had claimed that the Afar wore these trophies round their necks, but Thesiger reported that "they actually deny this and I find it difficult to believe that their denial is based on feelings of delicacy, when they are ready to admit that they will rip open a pregnant woman and mutilate the child inside her". Those unlucky warriors who returned empty-handed from a raid, he added, were "ragged unmercifully by their more successful companions, their clothes being soiled and cow dung rubbed into their hair".

It was not until April, 1934, that Thesiger and his party closed in on the Awash's missing outlet. When they reached the sultanate of Aussa, Thesiger could see the river entering a large, swampy lake called Adabada, "White Lake", after the colour of its water. Some comparatively peaceful Afar tribesmen whom he had persuaded to accompany him assured him that Lake Adabada had no exit. But Thesiger was not convinced. He climbed a hill and saw the Awash passing through two smaller lakes before disappearing to the west. His opinions thus confirmed, he determined to press on. For five days he waded through deep swamps "infested" with pythons to reach these lakes, and spent another two days crossing a belt of "cracked and riven lava" from the volcanic Mount Jira, the heat rising "as from a furnace door".

The trail led on to a third lake, Abhebad (now called Abbe), prized by the Afar for its supposed medicinal qualities. Thesiger remained on the treacherous black mud of its bare shores for seven days, checking for possible outlets. "Shade there was none, our drinking water was hot and brackish, and regularly at sunset a sandstorm swept down upon us from the Essa mountains across the lake," he wrote. By the seventh day, he satisfied himself that the lake had no exit. He had found the mouth of the Awash, 80 miles from the Red Sea. The river simply bled to death, evaporated in the middle of the desert. On May 20, 1934, near starvation point and after enduring almost six months in the scorching heat, he reached Tajura in French Somaliland and from there sailed home.

Few Europeans have walked the remoter parts of the Danakil since then, and I can claim to be one of them. However, I must admit I walked only briefly. I did most of my exploration from a height of some 50 feet, in a helicopter. Taking off from Tendaho at the centre of the Danakil, my pilot picked up the winding Awash as it flowed strongly eastwards, perhaps 70 yards wide, between steep muddy banks. A green strip of grass and acacia woodland stretched for about 100 yards on either side. Something slithered into the water as we approached—a crocodile about eight feet long. The muddy river is alive with crocodiles, but it is also well stocked with their staple diet, catfish, and the ample supply of food may explain why the Afar tribesmen fording the river with their camels and goats, cross without apparent fear or even watchfulness.

There were swamps along the river's course now. The helicopter put up a cloud of cattle egrets, and I spotted a horseshoe formation of great white pelicans dipping their heads rhythmically as they fished. A disgruntled hippo spouted a jet of water vapour from its nostrils and quickly scuttled itself. A second hippo, with a tangled clump of the water plant, Nile cabbage, perched incongruously on its head, sank more sedately, while its vegetable bonnet floated away.

We followed the course pioneered by Thesiger, and entered the Sultanate of Aussa where the river passes through the White Lake, which since Thesiger's time has become known as Lake Gamarri. As we continued north, the lakes and riverine woodlands of Aussa were soon left behind. The banks of the Awash became increasingly bare, grey lava showing through. The pace of the river quickened as it flowed along the foot of Mount Jira. More frequent white water appeared, then gave way to placid flow again. Suddenly the Awash broke up into several streams sluggishly flowing through banks of silt. The many-channelled waterway took on the look of a delta. It must have been about here that the tiring Thesiger began to guess how the river ended.

We were flying now only feet above the mud. The air blasting in through the open door of the cockpit smelled strongly acrid. Suddenly the pilot climbed to show me what lay ahead. A great shimmering lake appeared in the heart of the desert. This was the end the Awash was hurrying to meet. Lake Abbe, as Thesiger discovered, is a huge sump from which the waters of the river are sucked up by the sun as fast as the river can deliver them.

We turned south, heading back to Tendaho to refuel, this time over gritty lava deserts. Below, it was evident that other forms of life besides the Afar eke a living from the desert. A herd of 30 Soemmering's gazelle, a desert-adapted antelope, made the lava dust spurt at each hoof-fall as they galloped away before us. Wherever sparse clumps of grass managed to take hold, ostriches appeared, and in a rocky ravine stood one of the world's rarest creatures—the Somali wild ass, much like any donkey except that it is fatter and looks fitter. After we landed and refuelled at Tendaho, we set course north-west towards the Karum salt lake at the Danakil's far north-western corner. Beneath me was real Danakil country, lacking totally the green relief of the river Awash. Here along the Rift's north-south fault line, the lava's grey surface was interrupted with yellow, red and brown stains. I could not escape the impression that they were exhudations of a boil—matter ejected from beneath the skin of the sick earth.

It was from here that I took my short walk on one of the worst surfaces in the world, not from choice, but because fuel was running low. Finding a comparatively level spot on this craggy lavascape, we touched down. As we opened the helicopter door, the heat leaped up to meet us. The air was sulphurous and had an almost metallic taste. We stepped out. The volcanic crust crunched, fracturing like toughened glass beneath our weight. Indeed there was volcanic glass everywhere, lumps of brittle black obsidian. No human being, no matter how well his feet were pro-tected, could have walked more than a few hundred yards across this jagged lava, for it was burning hot. We were certainly not tempted. When we had poured more fuel into the main tank from cans inside the helicopter cockpit, we took off again as quickly as possible.

As we flew north towards the Red Sea coast, we followed the lie of the land downwards until we were flying nearly 400 feet below sea level. At this level we were enveloped in the blinding white expanse of the 45-mile-wide Karum salt lake, which was once part of the Red Sea. The salt is at least 3,700 feet deep. At first it was criss-crossed with cracks. It must have been wet quite recently and had then broken up as it dried.

The flat bottom of the Danakil desert, strangely lush during Ethiopia's brief but violent rainy season, glistens with water as the river Awash overflows to form a braid of narrow streamlets. The water spills down from the grassy high-lands, dividing and re-uniting around patchy thorn scrub in its path.
This annual wetting sustains the trees through the year, but the grasses that make this scene so green grow only for a brief period after the rains.

Farther on, glistening patches confirmed that quite a lot of water does reach this awful place. Heavy rains fall seasonally in the high plateau 50 miles to the west and, since water is bound ultimately to reach the land's lowest point, it comes here.

To my surprise, I saw that there were dots moving ahead of us on the salt crust. They were men from a completely specialized breed of Afar who, unlike most of their tribe, are both industrious and peaceful. They work with tools and methods of biblical simplicity, in temperatures often reaching 135 degrees Fahrenheit, levering the salt from the lake and chipping it with hand-tools into rectangular bars about the size of breeze blocks. Then the camel trains carry the salt bars to market at Makale in the distant highlands.

It is incredible that men would work most of their lives under such extreme conditions, but the Afar do not see it that way, although they receive only water and bread brought by the camel trains and the equivalent of a few shillings a day for their efforts. Salt provides them with all they need, even the building materials for their huts, which are made of salt blocks; it is used as money in various parts of Ethiopia, and an Englishman, Major Robert Cheesman, a former British consul in northwestern Abyssinia, has called Karum the Royal Abyssinian Mint. The reason for the high value of the salt is its scarcity on the high plateau of central Ethiopia. Cattle raised there have either to be driven long distances several times a year to places where they can get sufficient salt in their diet or fed bars of salt imported from Karum. The Afar clearly believe they are clinching arguments about the value of their produce when they comment that salt they can eat, but money they cannot.

Beyond the salt lake we came to a landscape equally inhospitable: deep gullies bordered with buttresses, the outermost ones standing alone, like rock pinnacles detached from a sea shore by eroding waves. Could water be the agent responsible here? It seemed highly possible. The pilot banked and headed down the only lane of order in a haphazard patterning of mud cliffs, a canyon in the bottom of which ran a trickle of rust-red ooze—more water, if it could be called that, from the highlands. Minarets and pinnacles, potholes and pits, crags and cliffs lined our route. The pilot hovered over a pit of brimstone whose green surface seemed to bubble. We were at Dallol, a huge dome disfigured by volcanic upheaval and contamination. It lies in the centre of the Karum plain, the heart of the heartless Danakil.

Suddenly we emerged from the canyon between a final group of buttresses and were back again in the blinding expanse of the salt. The helicopter curved around towards Tendaho for the return flight, passing a series of volcanoes. The flanks of the first one, nameless like so many features in this desert, belched yellow sulphurous smoke. The stench reached us even in the cockpit. Then another anonymous volcano appeared, with a crater so completely circular and sides so vertical that it might have been drilled with a brace and bit. For all its brand-new symmetry, it was apparently dormant. But the next volcano we flew alongside was certainly not. One part of its lip was torn away as if by a recent explosion, and we flew near enough to spot scarlet blossoms of molten fire in the lava at the bottom of the crater.

Our last Danakil experience was somewhat different, but no less disturbing. When we neared Tendaho, we came upon a cloud of steam rising from a boiling spring. As the steam parted in the downwash of the helicopter's blades, a man was revealed. He had the features of a bird of prey. He wore a white robe with a curved, double-edged knife at his belt and a rifle held behind his head and across his shoulders, hands looped over muzzle and bit.

He was an Afar, a Danakil warrior, and there was no expression of mercy or friendship in his face. He was unimpressed both by the intrusion and the retreat of the helicopter. He appeared almost scornful of it, scornful in the knowledge that while the machine and its occupants depended on the support of fuel and spare parts to exist in the barren expanses of the desert, he, alone, was utterly self-sufficient.

A Landscape of Salt

PHOTOGRAPHS BY DR. GEORG GERSTER

The great, dried-out expanse of the Karum salt lake in the Danakil Depression was once an arm of the Red Sea, from which its vast quantities of sodium chloride—sea salt—are mostly derived. It is entirely flat for the 45 miles of its width except at the centre, where volcanic buckling has raised a cluster of strangely contorted salt hills.

For most of the year, the salt lake is compact and glistening like marble but, when drenched by the short rains of late summer, it undergoes a strange metamorphosis. The marble-like surface softens and grows dull. Then, once more exposed to the powerful sun, it begins to dry out and shrinks rapidly, both horizontally and vertically. The horizontal contraction cracks off large hexagonal sections, five to six feet across, leaving gaps between. When the desert winds blow, these gaps may be filled by grains of gypsum, dust and sand, which harden like cement. In this case, as the salt hexagons continue to dry in the sun, shrinking downwards, the thin, dividing sections of harder materials are left upstanding in ridges (right). Gradually, however, the ridges are worn down by sand storms, and the smooth surface is finally restored.

The largest hill rising from the salt lake is Mount Dallol, an oval extrusion 125 feet high and two miles long at its base. Like the surrounding plain it is a structure of salt. It started as a gentle dome, raised by volcanic pressures deep within the earth, and bears a collapsed crater near the summit as evidence of these origins. The friable salt surface was later eroded by wind and water and shaped by dying volcanic activity, in the form of hot springs, into multi-coloured crags and sharp pinnacles.

The seasonal hot springs, or fumaroles, derive their water from the highlands bordering the Danakil Depression. The water drains down through cracks in the earth's crust and is heated by molten rock beneath. It is then forced, boiling, through mineral salt beds that give it colours. The boiling water spurts out of the earth in yellows, oranges and browns—the result of oxygen acting in various ways on iron deposits in the earth.

As the water cools, the salts crystallize, forming brilliantly coloured mounds among pools of green brine. The fumaroles last only a few months. As the water dries up, they fade to dull orange, then dirty grey.

The Karum salt lake stretches away as far as the eye can see, geometrically patterned as it dries and cracks after the summer rains. In time the raised ridges will disappear under the harsh, abrasive force of the desert wind.

Hot springs create these crags on Karum's Mount Dallol, spouting iron-yellow salt solution that overnight can dry into six-foot pinnacles.

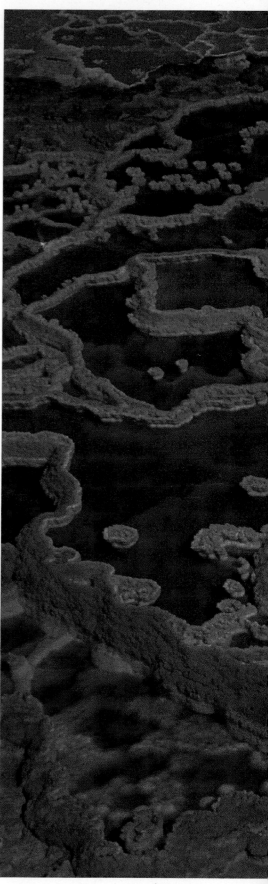

Pools of concentrated brine lie glassily between filagreed borders of yellow mineral salts near the crater on the top of Mount Dallol. Both the pools and their borders are created by the hot springs, or fumaroles, that spew salty water over wide areas of the hill.

When the water cools, it is trapped by its own salts, which gradually crystallize, layer after layer, and turn yellow from the iron they have picked up in the ground. As the water evaporates and becomes saltier, it turns progressively deeper shades of green.

Colour has faded from this grey fumarole on Mount Dallol, as it will from the other hot springs when their water supply diminishes.

Isolated chimney formations and vertical cliffs mark the ragged south-west corner of Mount Dallol. The chimneys are salt columns, up to 80 feet high. They were formed because their white caps of gypsum, a relatively insoluble mineral, diverted the eroding summer rains to the surrounding, unprotected salt, where deep gullies were eaten away.

Pinnacles of salt, chiselled by erosive
summer rains, bend up from the
glistening Karum salt lake (background).
Their needle-like shape contrasts with
the squat salt block (left in the picture)
which resisted erosion because it is
protected by a cap of less soluble gypsum.
The ringed pattern of both pinnacles
and block was formed as the salt
was deposited in layers over millennia.

3/ The Fish and the Fish-Eaters

You may note that the waters are Nature's storehouse,
in which she locks up her wonders.

ISAAK WALTON/ THE COMPLEAT ANGLER

Between the Danakil Desert on the Red Sea Coast and the more southern parts of the Rift Valley in Kenya and Tanzania lies the central tableland of Ethiopia, a volcanic mountain mass that dominates the whole country like a lion's paw holding down a toy landscape. In the north, the Rift first cleaves its way into this mass by means of the gorge of the river Awash. The progress southward of the Rift is marked for the next hundred miles by a group of four lakes, strung out along its centre line: Zwai, Langana, Abiata and Shala. Beyond are more lakes; Awausa, Abaya and Chamo. In Kenya the line is picked up and continued southwards through a chain of still more lakes, beginning with the greatest and most dramatic of them all, Lake Rudolf.

These lakes are the jewels that the Rift wears in its belt. Most are tainted with soda, some only slightly, others to such a degree that they are sumps of nearly pure sodium carbonate—washing soda. Only two are truly fresh—Baringo and Naivasha. The soda lakes support little but flamingoes—nearly three million of them, the largest concentrated mass of wildlife in the Rift. But the fresh and nearly fresh lakes are the ones that produce the most varied fauna, a fauna that ranges from crocodiles to hippos and hundreds of species of waterbirds including vast congregations of pelicans, kingfishers, herons, fish eagles and cormorants.

For most of these birds and certainly for the crocodiles, fish is a major item of diet. The main lakes that can be classed as less alkaline and therefore able to support numbers of fish and fish-eating animals are Rudolf in northern Kenya and the group, in the Ethiopian Rift Valley near Addis Ababa, which includes Shala and Abiata. The highest concentration of fish and fish-eaters occurs in fresh and only slightly bitter lakes—with one amazing exception.

The strangest tale of the Rift's fish-eaters concerns pelicans and their remarkable relationship to a lake that contains hardly any fish at all, even though its water is highly suitable for them. This is Shala, a remote, lovely, but sometimes intimidating place. Its name in the local Galla language means "pelican", and yet until very recently Europeans had never seen more than a few isolated pelicans on the lake. The mystery was compounded by the fact that Shala contains no fish apart from a few small ones, less than a couple of inches long, that gather around springs at the eastern end. The reason for this is that the lake is too deep and steep-sided to produce fish spawning grounds. Since pelicans are known to tuck away two or three pounds of large fish a day, the sparse supply of small ones could hardly be an adequate food source for even the few pelicans that had been seen. Where then did the pelicans on Shala feed and why, if there were only a few birds there, did the Galla tribesmen call the lake "Pelican"? The mystery was solved in 1969 when a Scotsman, Leslie Brown, one of the world's leading ornithologists, and an American zoologist, Dr. Emil Urban, of the Haile Selassie University in Addis Ababa, followed up a clue from an Ethiopian biologist, Ato Berhane Tessema. In the late 1950s Tessema had discovered something very interesting on one of Shala's more remote islands: pelicans were gathering there in large numbers. Plainly the Galla tribesmen, at some time in the distant past, had had an inkling of the birds' presence and named the lake after them.

Yet the knowledge had lapsed, and there is a good reason why the pelicans remained forgotten: the islands were not only remote, but virtually unobserved. Since there are no fish for human (or pelican) consumption, there are no native boats on the lake. The Galla do not go boating for mere pleasure, and outsiders who might have done so rarely visited the lake's western end, where the islands are located. These cannot be closely examined from the shore, since they lie well out in the lake, and heat-haze and mirage prevent an observer from making out anything but vague outlines, even with binoculars.

Once Brown and Urban had got their lead from Tessema they borrowed an aluminium cockleshell belonging to the Ethiopian Game Department and rowed out towards the island from the nearest point along the shore. This journey involved considerable danger, for the lake lies in a steep-sided bowl of hills down which savage winds can rip without warning; the two ornithologists were nearly capsized by several fierce squalls. But after several miles of rowing the risk was rewarded. On a flat, volcanic island of two-and-a-half acres, they found nearly 5,000 breeding pairs of great white pelicans. Until that moment it had been a mystery where the immense numbers of great whites in the northern part of the Rift did breed.

Before they dared begin studying them, Brown and Urban took considerable precautions. The pelicans must never know they were being overlooked, lest they desert their nests and abandon the island as a breeding place. The two men quietly departed and waited until the breeding season ended; then they returned to build a permanent hide in preparation for the following year. By the time the photographer, Dieter Plage, and I arrived at Shala, Brown and Urban had finished their researches and we were privileged to have the benefit of their knowledge and the use of their hide.

We made our journeys to what had come to be called Pelican Island from the eastern shore, covering the ten miles in a rubber boat with a powerful outboard, and every trip made me slightly apprehensive. On the northern shore, the rim of the bowl round the lake rises to a ridge over 3,000 feet above the lake surface. To the south the shore slope is not so steep, but close to the water's edge it drops more severely, and, having dropped, keeps on plunging straight down to make the water nearly 800 feet deep. This fact is somehow hard to forget several miles out on that dark blue surface. I always told myself that I could drown just as easily in eight feet of water as in 800, though somehow, on Shala, the thought is small consolation.

The first day we made the ten-mile trip, the hills that form the bowl of the lake were a rich green. The water, in one of its good moods, reflected the hills and sky so that it was hard to tell where the sky began and the hills ended. Flotillas of panicky little grebes skittered in front of the boat and then, when alarmed by our outboard, dived en masse and disappeared into the depths. White-winged black terns hunted for insects. Because Shala is so high, there is less atmosphere than normal to filter out the ultra-violet rays in sunlight, and these rays, reflected off the shining surface of the lake, were fearsome. The brilliant sun burned our skin. We quickly found that to prevent our lips from breaking open we needed to use protective grease.

Pelican Island emerged out of the haze very slowly. It is flat, like an

Great white pelicans, at ease on their breeding colony on Lake Shala, reveal that the bottom half of their immense beak is made of skin. When the pelicans submerge their heads during fishing, this flexible pouch distends to an enormous size, with a capacity of over two gallons of water, and serves as a scoop for catching the fish.

aircraft-carrier. The flight deck, where the pelicans nest, is at its southern end. The carrier's superstructure, marked by a gradual rise to a height of 30 feet above the waterline, is well aft of midships. On this grows the only tree, an acacia, the sole source of shade.

A lower fantail, about 50 yards long, drops away to the north. We took no chance of disturbing the birds, and began to turn to starboard in order to come round under the stern of the island at the safe distance of about one mile. Even this close it was difficult to make out more than a suggestion of white on a place where we knew anything up to 10,000 pelicans could be nesting.

While still 100 yards off Pelican Island we were hit by a smell only too familiar to bird enthusiasts: bird droppings or, to fertilizer companies, guano. We beached and pulled the boat well up on the grey lava sand; if a storm carried it away there would be no ferry service to pick us up. Outside the pool of shade from the lone acacia, sun, stench and rock-stored heat combined in an almost physical assault. We crept along the catwalk of lava behind the colony and, as we clambered up the slope into the hide built by Urban and Brown, the noise of the colony became deafening. The sound was not unlike the grunting of hippos.

Smell, noise and heat were all forgotten as we parted the sacking-covered slits of the look-out. At least 1,000 pairs of pelicans were nesting on a rocky plateau not more than 70 yards long by 50 wide; the nearest nests were less than five yards away from us. The colony was alive with activity as the birds milled around in the ritualized movements of courtship. Nearby, four males vying for the favours of a single, coy female thrust their beaks backwards and forwards in what Brown and Urban named "group knobber display"—they nicknamed breeding birds "knobbers" after the fatty knob, about the size of a billiard ball, that appears on the foreheads of both the yellow-faced males and pink-faced females a short time before they come into breeding pitch. At some distance a single male marched back and forth, showing off to a female in the "strutting walk".

There were young everywhere. Parties of up to a dozen greyish birds nearly as big as their parents had grouped together in "pods"; some were digging their heads deep into their parents' pouches to feed on pre-digested fish, scooping food from the very bottom of the avian shopping bag. The larger young dug with such ferocity that the sharp ends of their beaks sometimes caused punctures in the pouches.

Watching the feeding process, we pondered the second mystery of the pelicans that Brown and Urban had solved. At the time only about a

Captured at the instant of landing on its return from a day's fishing, a great white pelican spreads the flight feathers in the tips of its massive wings—they span nine feet—to reduce speed and make a neat, slow touchdown among its swimming companions, two adults and two young birds.

quarter of the potential nesting strength was in residence. Even so, enormous quantities of fish were being consumed each day. Later in the season, when all 5,000 nesting sites were occupied, this colony would require over three tons of fish a day to keep it going. If none of the food was to be found on Shala, the pelicans must clearly go elsewhere for it. But where? Looking around the lake, it was hard to imagine. The only easy exit was over the comparatively low shoreline to the south, but there are no fishing lakes anywhere within commuting distance of Shala in that direction. So the pelicans must have a route over the high bowl-like rim around the rest of the lake. How did they cross this barrier? To witness the solution to this mystery, we would have to wait until next day. It was late now and the pelicans were already settling down for the night. The evening breeze was blowing the lake into a short, nasty sea and we decided to call it a day and do the same as the birds. We left the cramped confines of the hide and pitched our tent well out of sight of the pelicans on the flat "fantail" of our aircraft carrier.

Early next morning, we watched with interest to see which way the pelicans would go when they set off to collect their daily food supply. About nine a.m., groups of adults took off and flew out into the lake—in the direction of the most challenging route, over the highest point of surrounding land, the 3,000-foot high, sharply-ridged peak we had seen on our voyage out. It was easy to guess where the pelicans were heading: Abiata, a lake well stocked with fish only ten miles away, over the mountains to the north. But to fly over the intervening peak would take time, and require a great deal of energy. Shortly, the pelicans demonstrated how they dealt with the problem. They were indeed going to fly over that peak. The first groups of adults that had taken off from the island landed on the water half-way to the peak. More small parties joined them until about 50 individuals were assembled. Then, as if at a signal, they took off together and flew low across the lake to the far shore. From Pelican Island we could just see the birds against the green-blue of the mountain-side. They had stretched out now and were wavering like a rope fixed at one end and shaken violently at the other. The mystery was solved. They were searching for a thermal, a rising current of hot air. Once they had found one, they would soar, like human glider pilots, effortlessly. As we watched, the birds found their thermal and started to spiral upwards on their ride over the mountain crest.

A great white pelican weighs up to 25 pounds and on the ground it appears a ludicrously clumsy bird. Yet once it starts to soar it becomes as agile as a sailplane. The thermalling birds corkscrewed up and up

An adult pelican, regurgitating the fish it has caught in a day's hunting, opens its beak to let a chick stretch its brown neck deep into the expansive parental throat.

until they were well above the crest of the mountain. If we could have flown with those birds, we would have seen Abiata stretching out ahead. This lake is full of fish, mainly tilapia, and the pelicans commute to it daily, using these thermal escalators.

Already another party had formed on the lake to take off for the mountain. As the first group reached maximum altitude, levelled out and started its ten-mile glide down to Abiata, the second began searching for an up-current, while third and fourth groups assembled on Shala. As the air warmed and soaring conditions improved, the outward air traffic increased, reaching a peak in early afternoon and then gradually tapering off. The birds that had climbed over the mountain to Abiata did not return with their catch for 24 hours.

Around ten a.m. those that had made the fishing trip the previous day started arriving back at Pelican Island. They, too, had had to wait for the air to heat up and provide thermal escalators—but on the Abiata side of the mountain—before they could attempt the return flight. The first party's arrival was announced by a whistle like that of a turbojet, as four pelicans, at least 500 feet above the island, planed down with wings half-closed, spilling air like a team of display parachutists. They dropped their paddles as air-brakes, side-slipping as they lost height, then levelled off and glided in at high speed to the centre of the colony, clapping their great wings to reverse their thrust before touching down. A throng of large youngsters was waiting, like relatives at an airport, and as soon as the first arrival, a rosy-faced female, had landed, one of them detached itself and chased after the food-laden adult. The female made its offspring pursue it for fully 15 yards before it relented and allowed the young bird to dip deep into the pouch for fish. No matter how crowded the nesting area, each parent unfailingly recognized its own young, or maybe vice versa.

Thermals on both sides of the mountain strengthened as the morning wore on. Outward and incoming traffic increased to match. By eleven, the swish of landing pelicans was continuous, each bird followed by a light snow-fall of soft, downy feathers, torn away by turbulence.

Now that we had witnessed the Shala end of the spectacle, we decided to go across to Abiata to watch the pelicans fishing. We made the long voyage back across Shala and early next day loaded our rubber boat on top of the Land Rover, then laboured up the rocky track between hillsides spiked with euphorbia trees, their candelabra branches lit with white flower flames. As we bumped and bounced along a roundabout, 30-mile route towards Abiata, shrouded in clouds of red dust, I could not help thinking of the ease and grace with which the pelicans reached the same goal.

The last four miles were across level savannah, beside a muddy stream. In the clear African morning sky, herons, ibis and cormorants passed overhead and hoopoes looped from tree to tree ahead of us. Mourning doves and laughing doves provided the perpetual savannah background of cooing and churring. It was nine a.m. and everything was taking a last deep, cool breath before the sun beat the life out of the day. Suddenly, at a widening of the stream, the peace was shattered by a chorus of harsh chortles. A thousand birds streaked across the bonnet of the Land Rover. Then, the whole grassland for a mile around exploded with golden-yellow birds. We stopped to watch, realizing that we had happened upon a great wildlife event.

The birds were all chestnut-bellied sandgrouse. A long period of drought in the area had brought them from many miles around to the one stream whose course we were following, to a solitary shelving beach. The first parties came in ahead of our vehicle, touched down a few yards from the water on the sandy beach and then immediately took off around an acacia tree half-way along the beach. It was all very orderly, with no pushing or risk of aerial collision. The chortle of birds arriving on one side of the acacia was almost blotted out by the wing-roar of those departing on the other. To stand at the edge of the beach was almost frightening. The sheer impetus and noise of the bird-flow had some of the characteristics of a jet engine. I had never seen anything quite so audibly and visibly impressive.

The four to nine sips of water each bird took are all that is needed to sustain it throughout a day of seed-gathering in the burned-up bush. I watched the male birds, those with pronounced bands on their chests, to see if they fluffed out their breasts as they drank. During the breeding season, the males trap water in specially adapted breast feathers so that they can carry water back to the young, and the young then "milk" the liquid from the feathers. But these birds were clearly drinking for themselves alone, so they could not have had young.

The traffic was easing off now. I glanced at my watch. Exactly six-and-a-half minutes after it all began, the last bird faded away against the hills and the savannah was left to two speckled pigeons. We had watched about 50,000 sandgrouse take their daily drink.

We drove on to Abiata, across grassy flats where crowned and Caspian plovers searched for insects. At last we launched our boat and set out towards the pelicans' fishing spot. This had taken Leslie Brown and Emil Urban nearly a year to discover. They had expected the birds to land exactly where they did their fishing, but in fact only a small percentage do so. Most touch down elsewhere and then swim to the fishing grounds. The most favoured spot lies where a stream flows into an area of dead trees that were killed by a recent rising in the level of the lake. This flooded woodland serves as an angling centre for all the other kinds of birds that recognize the fishiness of Abiata: kingfishers, cormorants, darters and all kinds of heron, including spear-fishing goliaths and the black herons that make a circular sunshade with their wings and catch tiddlers beneath. Each tree was decorated with the untidy, guano-plastered nests of the cormorants and darters, which had chosen to breed near the fish-market, so to speak. I came to think of this place as a waterbird city.

Into this city come the great white pelicans from Shala, arriving every morning in commuter relays. When they fish, they do so in flotillas, dipping their beaks in unison like rowers bending to the oars. They drive the fish into the shallows to be more easily caught. Of 40 or more birds fishing together, only a handful are successful each time, throwing back their heads to swallow the catch. Next day, with at least two pounds of tilapia stowed away, they will face the long climb back up the thermal escalator to Pelican Island on Lake Shala. It seems an arduous journey for the pelicans to undertake but, unlike the cormorants and darters of waterbird city, great white pelicans demand complete seclusion before they are prepared to nest. Pelican Island on fishless Lake Shala gives them precisely the privacy and freedom from interruption that they need. It is their only nesting colony in a thousand miles of the northern part of the Rift Valley.

There is far less mystery, though there are some surprises, surrounding those other wholesale fish-eaters of the Rift Valley lakes—the crocodiles. Perhaps the most surprising thing is their localized distribution. They require constant warm temperatures, so a high altitude lake such as Naivasha, at over 6,000 feet, with occasional morning frosts, is not for them. They demand sandy shores, secure from intrusion, on which the females can bury their eggs at breeding time. In modern times only two Rift lakes satisfy all these conditions. Baringo, which is full of tilapia, has a still large but decreasing crocodile population. Lake Rudolf, and the river Omo which flows into its northern end, is the main crocodile stronghold. Rudolf is estimated to hold 12,000 crocs.

This great population is mainly attracted by the lake's ample supplies of Nile perch, the largest fish found in the Great Rift Valley. A hundred-pounder is worthy of only passing comment. The great fish, bright silver, with a strange eye that hides its pupil and looks like a pale yellow glass marble, has the sharp, upstanding dorsal spines of the fresh-water perch and the sea bass. I have fished for Nile perch both with a spinning lure from the shore and by trailing a six-inch plug or large spoon from a boat. As a sporting proposition they are not so exciting as their size might suggest, especially on the tackle generally used here, which is more suited to shark. On a light rod the bigger fish fight dour and deep, but without any special display of fireworks.

The main breeding ground for crocodiles in Lake Rudolf is Central Island, a small cluster of volcanic craters that acts as a sanctuary for reptiles in the same way that Pelican Island does for pelicans on Lake Shala. It is a frightening place with a feeling of the lost world about it. There are no pterodactyls here, but crocs themselves are virtually pre-historic, for they have remained almost unchanged for 130 million years. They breed mainly on the flat and seldom-visited shores of two of its three water-filled craters, one of which is connected to the lake.

I had flown over the crater lakes before I made the choppy, fifteen-mile journey to the island by small boat. What struck me was that the water in each has a different colour: brown, green and blue. The phenomenon remains constant in all cloud and lighting conditions, so the explanation must lie in the craters themselves. Possibly, different depths or bottom formations encourage separate algal growths, but I could not be sure of this even when I finally visited Central Island.

As soon as I landed on the beach, I noticed a series of deep, sinuous grooves cut into the black lava sand by the tails of large saurians crawling ashore. On the shores of the main crater lake I discovered a strange notice. It said: "Lake A. No fishing. No shooting." It was, I believe, erected by the local fisheries officer, Bob McConnell, at Ferguson's Gulf, halfway up the western shore of Rudolf, in the certain knowledge that only a score of eyes, apart from those of the crocodiles, herons and egrets, would ever see it. It must be one of the loneliest jokes in the world.

The loneliness was made sinister by the knowledge that the crocodiles here can on rare occasion be aggressive. On Central Island and elsewhere in Lake Rudolf, they normally take little notice of humans. I have often swum in the tepid, soda-slippery waters of the lake with no more than a small element of risk. However, the rule has its exceptions. The one scientist—to my knowledge—who has spent any length of time

A Rudolf crocodile closes its jagged jaws on a dead cichlid fish. Acting as both predators and scavengers, these mighty reptiles ambush animals, usually herbivores like antelope, at the water's edge, and make short work of any carcases—like this one—that they find drifting on the surface.

doing field research into the flora and fauna of Central Island was bitten by one of his case studies, though he survived.

When crocs are around I tread with a good deal of caution, though when disturbed on land they are most likely to flee back to water. However, there is always a chance of meeting the exception, perhaps a big croc who is feeling the pangs of hunger. Crocodiles catch most of their prey in the water though they sometimes lie in wait on game trails leading to favourite drinking places to snatch a young or careless antelope by the leg. So I kept a wary eye on a ten-footer basking, with mouth open to cool himself, higher up the shore and between myself and the water. This reptile was more worried about me than I was about it. Persecution everywhere has made crocodiles extremely wary. Suddenly it raised itself on stiff legs and galloped back to the lake, entering with a crash like a torpedo. There it lay, looking like a sunken log, eyes just above the surface. I recalled hunters' tales about how basking crocs knock their prey from the bank and into the water with a lash of their tails. Even though I know there is no truth in the story—it is a physical impossibility—I gave the reptile a wide berth. There is something that defies reason about crocs.

Rudolf crocodiles are usually docile, yet for some unexplained reason, crocodiles are highly aggressive in the Omo and other rivers to the north of the lake flowing down from the Ethiopian highlands. While I was there, an 18-footer swallowed a man in the river Baro. When it was shot 24 hours later and cut open, only the legs of the victim were still recognizable. Apart from their different natures, there is one small physical distinction: Rudolf crocodiles grow a horny nodule on the belly skin, perhaps because of the lake's alkalinity (in the long run this may prove to be to their advantage, since it makes their skin less desirable commercially). But their vastly different behaviour is probably accounted for by the abundance in the lake of large Nile perch. Crocodiles are great fish-eaters and eaters of great fish in particular. A 50-pound Nile perch that is easily caught gives a fair return for crocodile effort. As a result, the Rudolf croc has far less need to dine on human prey. Faced with a shortage of fish, however, the reptile would almost certainly be as dangerous as its Omo neighbour.

The only other large population of crocodiles in the Rift is at Lake Baringo, 120 miles south of Rudolf. It has no Nile perch but great quantities of tilapia and barbus live in its fresh waters, and the air temperature at 3,000 feet is well suited to the saurians. The animals prosper in this favourable environment, and their disposition is usually even more amiable than that of the Rudolf crocodiles. Njemps tribesmen sometimes stand shoulder-deep far out in the lake, calmly fishing for tilapia while crocodiles on a similar mission swim close by.

This crocodiles' lake has a special interest of its own. The strange thing about Lake Baringo is that it remains fresh. Its neighbours to the south—Hannington, Nakuru and Elmenteita—are soda lakes, and it is surrounded by much the same volcanic countryside as they are. Moreover, Baringo has no visible outlet, through which the toxic minerals that affect its companions can wash away.

The explanation was first discovered by that pioneer geologist of the Rift, J. W. Gregory. He believed that Baringo had once been drained by a large river flowing from its northern end towards Lake Rudolf, 120 miles away. Among the many phenomena he noted was a geological difference between the two ends of the lake. On the northern shore was a mass of rocky outcrops and headlands, whereas the southern shore consisted of a sedimentary plain. When he inspected the plain more closely, he discovered that it too contained rocky outcrops, only here they had been buried by subsidence and then covered with sediment washed down from the surrounding hills. From this observation Gregory concluded that during some ancient upheaval of the Rift the whole lake had tilted, so that the northern end was raised and the southern lowered. These movements, together with the lava flows that accompanied them, cut the northern river. Gregory believed that the outlet, so essential to the lake's freshness, remained where it had been, at the northern end, but underground. He recorded that he had seen water seeping away through the crumbly lava flows there.

Today there is no sign of a subterranean outlet or even a clue to one until a place called Kapedo, 70 miles to the north. Here may lie the explanation of Baringo's freshness. In the midst of dry, hot and barren country, Kapedo is an oasis. complete with doum palms and a waterfall tumbling over a 30-foot cliff. The water steams. At first I took this steam for spray, yet the fall is not high enough to produce a spray mist. When I got closer I found that the tumbling water really was steaming. It emerges from thermal springs and is close to boiling point.

Both the heat and the very existence of the water at Kapedo hint that it flows underground from Baringo. 70 miles away. This underground link is by no means as improbable as it might seem at first. Water penetrates the complicated system of lake sediments, volcanic ash and old porous lavas on the floor of the Rift as if they were made of

*With graceful precision, a fish eagle
plucks a meal from the weedy fringes of
its home lake. Sighting a fish near the
surface, the eagle glides down, fanning
its tail and slotting its wingtips to
prevent stalling (below). With a snatch
of the talons and a great downstroke of
the wings, it lifts its prey clear (bottom),
beats hard to gain height (centre) and
banks away to a feeding perch (far right).*

APPROACH

SNATCH

SPRINT

BANKING

STABLE FLIGHT

sponge. Moreover, the recent thermal activity beneath the Rift would heat the underground river. Nearby is an extinct volcano called Silali whose subterranean fires may still be smouldering.

The same explanation, an underground outlet, almost certainly accounts for the freshness of Lake Naivasha, 150 miles south of Baringo. Like Baringo, Lake Naivasha is fed by streams flowing in from a volcanic catchment area. Yet its waters remain beautifully fresh for the same reason. The best guess is that the all-essential leak occurs at the southern end of the lake. In the days when the level of water in the Rift was much higher and the lake far larger than it is today, an overflowing river certainly poured out from this end. The lie of the ground certainly falls away most steeply from here, descending 5,000 feet to the next lake, Magadi, about 120 miles to the south. So perhaps Naivasha's secret seepage is through the crumbly lavas in the direction of that austere, soda-encrusted lake.

At an altitude of 6,200 feet, Naivasha is not only the highest lake in the Rift, it is possibly the most beautiful and certainly the finest aviary. Here is Africa's largest concentration of nesting fish eagles, the great bronze and white birds whose cry, a spine-tingling, fluting whistle, has been called the Sound of Africa. The eagles live on the lake's thriving population of tilapia and black bass. The tilapia were introduced by Europeans when they settled in East Africa a century ago and desired good eating. The black bass were brought from North America as predators to eat the tilapia when this species grew too numerous for the lake. Since both species swim near the surface and are an ideal size for large fish-hunting birds, they quickly attracted the fish eagles. Meanwhile, other smaller fish support a thronging population of lesser predators from herons to kingfishers.

The setting that Naivasha provides for this concourse of water birds is one of the finest in the Rift. The lake is nearly circular and its fresh, crystal waters lie cupped within four mountainous walls: to the south rises the green bulk of the great volcano, Longonot; to the west, the Mau escarpment, which forms one wall of the Rift; to the north, the buttress of the dead Eburu volcanoes; to the east, the Kinangop plateau, which climbs to the Aberdare mountains and forms the eastern wall of the Rift. As Baringo is brown and bare, so Naivasha is lush and green for, being higher, it is cooler and more moist. Flat-topped acacia trees stand upon its shores; in its shallows and drifting about the lake are immense beds of papyrus; the purple lotus flowers of water lilies create an air of tranquil pleasure. But the calm can be deceptive. When the

Perched on a reed stem, a malachite kingfisher holds a live fish firmly in its bill. In the midst of its headlong catching dive, the bird was content merely to seize the fish. Now it must find a way of swallowing its prey without choking on fins and scales. With quick flicks of the head it will thrash the fish against the perch to kill it, then flip the corpse round to swallow it head-first.

rainy season's cumulus clouds bank high over the Rift Valley walls, the wind can come spilling off the heights, rushing down with the power of an unseen avalanche, whipping a smiling surface into a black fury, cratering the lake with meteorites of hail and giant raindrops. Such a wind overturns the fronds of floating lily-leaves and makes even the ten-foot-high papyrus stems bend like grass.

At first glance it seems that there are fish eagles scattered about in practically every attractive nesting or look-out tree, especially the acacias. But the arrangement is far from haphazard. Each pair of birds commands a rectangle of fishing and nesting territory that stretches out over the lake. Any other eagle fishes inside this area at its peril. Sometimes the territories lie side by side, like neighbouring, but rival, states. Even so, there is no trespassing. Moreover, since the rectangles stretch only a certain distance from the shore, the open waters in the centre of the lake are, so to speak, international, like the oceans. Any eagle can fish there. If it were not for this convention, the young birds would fare badly, since their parents will not tolerate them inside parental waters once they have become self-supporting fish-catchers. The birds' distinctive call is usually made to proclaim ownership of territory and sometimes to challenge a rival eagle. Often it is the trespassing bird that throws out the challenge, gracefully flinging back its white head and neck in mid-flight to do so.

The eagles exhibit the same elegant power when they fish, a remarkable display of co-ordinated action that I have often been lucky to watch. I was standing on the edge of Naivasha on one occasion when a male called from the top of a stark tree that had been killed by a temporary rising of the lake's level. (I knew it was a male because its cry was shriller than its mate's—the male is the treble, the female the contralto.) I saw it just before it struck at its prey. At the surface of the water, the movement of a black bass's dorsal fin had caught its attention. The eagle launched itself in a long, low, curving pass. At the last moment it threw its legs well forward, hooking talons into the fish, which weighed at least two pounds. For a fraction of a second the weight of the fish almost stopped the great bird in the air, but its flight was barely checked—some calculate that eagles strike with the energy equal to that stored in a bullet from an elephant rifle. Sheer impetus dragged the fish out of the water and, in a second, the eagle was swinging back to the trees with the fish held beneath. The bass's fins flapped feebly as it was carried, helpless, in those fish-hook claws.

The fish-eagles are the bird stars of Naivasha but they are backed by a magnificent and colourful supporting avian cast. Innumerable other birds live here as well: superb and glossy starlings; little parrot-like love-birds; green wood-hoopoes probing for insects in holes made by wood-boring bees; Nubian and Cardinal woodpeckers hammering so fast that it is a wonder their skulls can stand the vibration; lilac-breasted rollers swooping with a flash of electric blue about their wings. For brilliance they are rivalled only by a kingfisher that seldom, if ever, fishes, preferring to eat grasshoppers, lizards and insects. This is the woodland kingfisher, a nester in deserted woodpecker holes, a grey-headed, greenish-blue dandy found sometimes by water, but, as the name implies, more often among the trees. The woodland kingfishers can be seen swooping down to dead trees out in the shallows, disappearing inside the old woodpecker holes to feed their young chicks or perhaps to prospect for nesting sites.

All these tree-nesting bird species find specialized niches within the habitat created by acacias and lakeside bush. But right beside them are two quite different watery habitats, each supporting its own specialized bird population. On the lake itself, life is organized into two quite separate kingdoms: those of the papyrus islands and lily beds.

Papyrus is the plant from which the ancient Egyptians made paper, and it also formed the so-called "bulrushes" among which Moses was said to have been found. Papyrus is most certainly not a bulrush but a giant sedge, as its tough, triangular-sectioned stem shows. The plant grows in dense clumps that may resemble firm islands, but it is only necessary to set foot on them to discover that they are far from solid land. The space between the matted papyrus roots and the silted bottom of the lake is dead space, lacking sufficient dissolved oxygen to support aquatic life. Luckily for life on the lake bed, the papyrus is always on the move, sailing before the inconstant winds of the Rift, island joining with island to form archipelagos, continents and sub-continents encircling minor oceans of their own making.

The stems and flowerheads of the papyrus afford admirable fishing vantage points and cover for all manner of water birds. The malachite kingfisher makes flashing dives from the papyrus stems into gaps among the lily pads, spattering droplets of water. This bird is only four inches long, but its tiny size intensifies the brilliant blue of its body so that it becomes a glimmering gem. Another species, the pied kingfisher, scarcely seems to need a resting-place at all, for it can hover like a kestrel and does so for the same reason: to pinpoint its prey. It always seems to

An adult squacco heron rests quietly on a bending papyrus stem before resuming its search for food. For much of the day, it picks a delicate path through the waterside vegetation, patiently awaiting the movement that will betray its prey among the jungle of tangled roots and towering papyrus. Then it will pause briefly to snap up some aquatic insect or larva, perhaps even a small fish or frog.

make several fruitless dives for every tiddler it snatches from just below the surface. Perhaps its shadow gives it away.

The papyrus fulfills a different function for the herons, which know what all good fishermen know: that, to be unseen by the fish, it is vital to pick a background with which one merges. On Lake Naivasha, the papyrus stems perfectly suit the colour of the purple, grey and goliath herons. Five feet tall, the goliath is the largest heron in the world. In contrast, diminutive squacco herons can be seen crouched on the papyrus edges, waiting motionless, minutes on end, for tiddlers to swim within range. Mostly, though, these small herons hunt unseen, dining off the numerous tree frogs. Little egrets and cattle egrets share the hunting ground, clinging to the swinging papyrus stems. At lake level, black crakes creep secretively among the roots.

On the lily beds live the tight-rope artists of the lake, birds that know precisely how much weight a lily leaf will bear as they stalk across its quaking surface in search of insects and larvae. For the smallest inhabitants, weight presents no problem. The African pied wagtail is so slight that its bobbing progress does not depress a lily pad by a centimetre. For the smaller waders, too, sandpipers of many species, weight creates few problems. Larger waders like ruffs (the males) and reeves (the females of the same species) are just heavy enough to have to hurry over the lily pads if they do not wish to get their feet wet.

The king of the lily pads is the bird whose popular name sums up an evolutionary history devoted to solving the problems of travel on this swaying habitat—the lily-trotter, or jacana. It is a moorhen-sized bird, chestnut-coloured, with blue head and bill, weighing about a pound. Most of its life is spent afloat on lily leaves. It not only feeds on them, but finds safety there for itself and its young family. The ability to move freely on the lily pads depends upon its outsize feet with enormously elongated toes, the perfect adaptation to this strange environment. These feet spread the bird's weight across the largest possible area and thus the plant on which the lily-trotter trots can remain afloat. I have watched with wonder as a female leads newly hatched young across the lily beds of Naivasha. At first I did not realize that the hen had chicks with her, until I looked more closely and saw four stick-like pairs of legs hanging down beneath her closed wings. Almost from the moment of hatching, the lily-trotter's chicks are expected to accompany their mother when she walks upon the water. The moment they leave the nest, the lily pads become their natural world. But there is no shelter for them if a sudden storm, or a predator like a marsh harrier, catches the family in the open. In an emergency, the parent calls the young to her. They hop up to her side. The parent clamps her wings over them and lifts them off their feet, giving them warmth and protection. The hen moves about with her family until the moment of danger has passed. Then she simply opens her wings and releases the young to learn for themselves the art of lily-trotting.

Naivasha is perhaps unsurpassed in its softness and beauty by any of the other lakes of the Rift. Here the beauty is not just in the landscape, but in the whole wild world that awakes and returns to sleep every day. In the golden sunlight of an African morning, there is dew on the grass and occasional patches of frost, too. The purple lotus flowers of the water lilies are not open yet. There is not a sound except a fussing of coots around the lily pads. The wide lily beds silently tremble and lift above the backs of fish searching for crustacea, snails and larvae on the ceiling of their green underworld. Then a black crake tiptoes out of the papyrus and a pair of African pochard plane in, wings set and paddles down, scratching the glassy surface with their landing. Gradually, the lake assumes the throbbing vitality of the daytime.

The hour of greatest beauty is the one just before nightfall. Dusk on the equator is a rapid dimming. Long before the light goes down, the purple lotus flowers of the lily beds have closed again. Yet a Naivasha sunset grows its own blooms. Skeins of egrets, ducks, geese and pelicans blossom against the purpling dusk that clings to the Rift Valley walls. And a million tree frogs tune up to sing their nocturne.

NATURE WALK / # Through Hell's Gate

Within an almost continuous basin of escarpments and volcanic hills, left behind by the contortions of the Rift over the past 16 million years, lies Lake Naivasha, still large but much reduced from its ancient size. One of its old outlets seems to have been a narrow, dramatic serpentine pass that is now called, with some justification, Hell's Gate. The pass falls away southwards from Naivasha's 6,200-foot altitude, abutting the west flank of the great volcano Longonot, whose lava once dammed the waters of prehistoric Naivasha. In this gorge twisting through the mountain wall lie a multitude of habitats and some spectacular rock formations, an extraordin-

arily vivid cross-section in miniature of Rift geology and wildlife.

On an early March day, with a high-altitude haze that precedes the rainy season taking some of the sting out of the sun, I set out to follow the one-time route of the lake's turbulent escape through Hell's Gate. It would still be hot by any standards, so I wore a wide-brimmed sun-hat and carried a water bottle that I was determined not to use until my thirst really persuaded me.

Starting down the lake shore towards the pass, I walked at first parallel with Longonot, picking my way along the edge of a dense papyrus thicket. The spiked flower heads of the towering sedges shut me off from the cool world of water. I could hear the trombone solos of hippos grunting and snorting in the shallows beyond, but the great animals themselves were entirely hidden from me by the bankside vegetation. Every now and again I was able to snatch a glimpse of the water of the lake through a gap in the papyrus, where hippos came ashore to wander in search of their nightly rations of lake-side grasses.

Over the centuries, hippos have learned that it is only safe to venture ashore to seek their food after

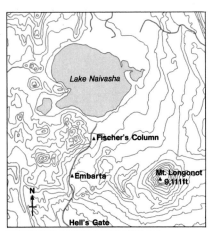

THE ROUTE THROUGH HELL'S GATE

THE VOLCANO LONGONOT ABOVE HELL'S GATE PASS

dark. They first learned the lesson in the days when Africans hunted them with spears for food. The arrival of Europeans and their fire-arms made daylight foraging even more perilous. From that moment on, they were shot for so-called sport and—with more justification—because they conflicted with farming interests. No one shoots them at Naivasha now, but the hippos still have their inborn sense of caution.

I followed one of the tracks made by the animals. Hippos are great path-makers, sometimes covering as much as 20 miles in a night. They move like bulldozers through the thickest scrub, though their trails are surprisingly narrow. There is no passing room in the tracks, and when I follow one I always hope that I will not be unlucky enough to meet a hippo coming in the opposite direction, for of all the dangerous animals encountered in the African bush, a hippo is one of the most lethal. Each jaw is armed with 30-inch ivory tusks and the mouth has the gape of an earth-grab. These monstrous weapons are likely to be used if a hippo is caught on land, for it is then a frightened animal. Its one thought is to return to the safety of the water. It weighs well over a ton, and can touch 20 m.p.h.; the result can be fatal. I was counting on the fact that the Naivasha hippos seldom venture ashore in daylight, but I was relieved to get into open country.

I turned my back on the cool lake scene of Naivasha and approached Hell's Gate. Immediately I was amidst a stand of trees whose grey bark

FEVER TREE

STAR GRASS

was peeling off, revealing a fresh surface that appeared bright yellow in the sunlight. They were *Acacia xanthophloea*, which the early European settlers called fever trees, a misnomer, and an unfair one—these acacias grow at the waterside where the settlers often caught malaria, so the trees were blamed for the disease before the anopheles mosquito had been identified as the culprit.

Beyond the fever trees, a mile-wide stretch of savannah—a yellow expanse of star grass dotted with

ANT-HOLE IN WHISTLING THORN

stunted bushes of whistling thorn—funnels towards the gorge entrance. The whistling thorn belongs to the acacia family, as do 80 per cent of the trees in the arid plains country of the Rift. But this variety has its peculiarities. On one I noted a large clear globule of sap, the first I had seen on any acacia. More distinctive of this type, however, are its dark round galls. Ants burrow into the galls and through the holes they make, the wind whistles sharply; hence the name for the tree.

But the ants also do the thornbush a service: the formic acid they secrete acts as an irritant to the muzzles of browsing animals. Thus there is a mutually beneficial relationship between these two incongruous parties, the ants getting nourishment from the galls and, in exchange, protecting the thornbush from rhino, giraffe and antelope.

Although the country around Hell's Gate has little game—which has almost vanished from most of the heavily farmed areas on the valley floor—the gorge itself forms a natural refuge for animals, small and large. Just before I entered the savannah funnelling into it, a reedbuck with ridged, back-curving horns sprang nervously from a thick tangle of cover, giving me a far greater fright than I gave it. There were grey duiker in the undergrowth too—tiny antelopes that are almost as small as hares. The name means "diver" in Afrikaans, and accurately describes the plunging, hare-like manner in which these graceful little

THORN-TREE SAP

OSTRICHES—TWO MALES AND A FEMALE—ON THE ALERT

animals dip and scamper at speed.

Another antelope, a dik-dik, so minute that it might almost have been a toy, froze as its keen ears caught my footfall. Dik-dik, which usually weigh no more than ten pounds, will stand immobile for as long as 20 minutes if a predator such as a martial eagle, the most powerful of all Africa's eagles, should perch nearby, or cast its ominous, brief shadow as it drifts past. But I did not pose a comparable threat, so the dik-dik decided to make a run for it.

Deep now in the savannah, I saw a grey line to my right that at first appeared to be a cloud shadow. Binoculars revealed a herd of 30 zebra; their vertically-striped camouflage had blended perfectly into the mirage shimmering over the sea of yellow grasses.

On the outskirts of the main zebra herd I now spotted a small family party, the stallion a little apart and watchful over his mares. One mare had a young foal. The stallion spotted me and whistled in alarm. The mare moved in front of her foal which bucked playfully, a charming toy animal, looking like a mint humbug in his baby stripes.

The zebra were accompanied by seven ostriches, a combination that at first seems bizarre. It is, however, quite usual. The alert ears of the zebra combine in an alliance of senses with the ostriches' eyes—another example of a mutually advantageous interchange of talents. What the zebras do not hear or scent, the ostriches see. Since what alarms and threatens one species also alarms and threatens the other, each of the oddly assorted partners acts as an early-warning system for the other.

Entrance to the Gorge

To the west now, the immense guardian buttress of Hell's Gate loomed high up in front of me. I passed another thorn tree, which like many of the taller acacias had untidy clumps of dried grasses wedged in its upper branches. These are the

WEAVERS' NESTS IN THORN TREE

WEAVER BIRD

nests of a small bird, Reichenow's weaver, canary yellow and, in the male, marked by a black back and matching eye-patches. Like all weavers, it is a highly-skilled thatcher of twigs and grasses. As I watched, one of the birds alighted alongside its nest and darted inside.

If Hell's Gate was a refuge for birds and game, it was also a hunting ground for predators and scavengers. Death and its attendants are never far away in the African grasslands. Leopards, eagles, civets and small cats such as serval all take their toll of small mammals. Where there is death there is a need for undertakers. Vultures are the principal functionaries, but mammals, like the pair of jackals that stalked boldly across my track, also do their bit. Some people dismiss jackals as slinking, skulking creatures. Perhaps they are when scrapping over a carcass with hyenas. Then they know their place. But these were untroubled by opposition, and trotted by as confidently as handsome dogs.

The jackals had barely disappeared from sight when a great grey bird came parachuting over the lip of the gorge, legs dangling a full two feet beneath its body. At first sight, it might have been taken for a stork. It was in fact a secretary bird, which is something of an oddity in the animal world. This bird of prey is the only species in a family known as the *Sagittariidae*.

After its apparently ungainly, but controlled descent, the secretary bird touched down and began to strut along as if the need to fly had never occurred to it. Indeed, it is fairly rare to see the secretary bird in the air. It is usually glimpsed stalking with slow, dignified gait on black legs that make the bird seem attired in plus fours. The bird's stalk is generally purposeful: brushing aside the grasses, it keeps an eye open for snakes, lizards and small rodents. The one I was watching certainly did. Its hooked beak struck and came up with a small lizard. Another time the victim might easily have been a puff-adder, for snakes, poisonous or harmless, are among the secretary bird's favourite meals.

The secretary bird in action against a snake is unbelievably fast. The bird uses its strong legs and taloned feet to strike the fatal blows. The length of its legs seems to keep it out of harm's way. Throughout the

SECRETARY BIRD

attack it remains tensed to spring aside or to take off. The blows come in quick succession. I once watched a cobra subdued in this fashion. Quick-striking though a cobra is, it just did not have a chance. Within 20 blows the snake was dead. The bird I now watched swallowed its lizard and continued in search of something more satisfying.

Suddenly, a small rich-brown antelope with a black stripe along its flank zig-zagged across the track. It was a Thomson's gazelle. Where there is one, there is usually a party. A sweep with the binoculars disclosed a number of black spikes poking up through the grass. The spikes might easily have

THOMSON'S GAZELLES

been dead grass stems, but when they moved, they did so in pairs. They were horns. Fifteen "Tommies" were lying down, relaxing while they digested their early-morning meal. They were not exclusively a stag party, for Thomson's gazelles, unlike most species of antelope have horns regardless of sex.

By the side of the track grew leonotis, tall plants with a succession of flower-heads spaced along the stems, each flower-head sprouting slender, reddish blossoms. A small gemlike creature, a male scarlet-chested sunbird, probed the inside of the trumpets with its long curved beak. The bird was dazzlingly iridescent, the brilliant red of its throat setting off the shimmering metallic green of its head and neck. In delicacy of form and sheer brilliance, Africa's sunbirds are a match for the New

A LEONOTIS FLOWER

World's hummingbirds. Both are nectar eaters, though the sunbirds lack the hummers' ability to hover. On another nearby leonotis perched a small black and white hunting bird, a fiscal shrike. Shrikes use such look-out points to spot their victims —insects and small rodents mainly.

Suddenly, as the rock walls of the gorge began to hem me in, a sound like tearing calico burst on my ears

FISCAL SHRIKE ON LEONOTIS

and a formation of miniature black jets passed barely three feet away. They were Nyanza swifts. They climbed nearly vertically to the centre of the rock wall and then most of them simply disappeared among a hundred thousand crannies. The whole rock face was alive with shrieking swifts. It was clearly a paradise for them, for the trees and grass were full of insects, which they were busily snatching from midair. The hissing of cicadas was everywhere.

Suddenly there was a loud, yelping cry. Those swifts still in flight scattered in panic. Some dived towards the grassland. Most darted straight at the rock face at a speed approaching 80 miles an hour. In the last yard of headlong flight, they braked abruptly and miraculously found perches. But one intrepid party mobbed the source of the

alarm, a black Verreaux's eagle.

The swifts need not have been so concerned by the intruder. The gorge provides food galore in the form of small mammals for this and many other birds of prey. Only a few moments before I had seen an augur buzzard hovering and then swooping on something in the grass—a mole rat perhaps, or even a wingless grasshopper like the one at my feet.

The swifts made high-speed passes within feet of the eagle's ferocious beak and talons. But the great bird soared along the cliff face unperturbed—its only concession to being buzzed was an imperious left and right bank that was more a shrug than a defence against these trivial irritants. Then the swifts returned to their insect-hawking.

The western bastion of Hell's Gate begins as a gentle, grass-covered in-

WINGLESS GRASSHOPPER

cline above a few yards of naked, vertically faulted rock. The slope climbs so steeply that, within 100 yards, the rock face is already 100 feet high. Wall and slope continue to soar until they level off at about 300 feet. The vertical columnar pattern of this immense cliff is repeated many times in the Rift. It is a fault scarp, one of the innumerable minor rendings and sinkings of the floor along the trough of the valley.

At a point that must have been midstream when Naivasha's waters rushed through Hell's Gate stands an imposing pinnacle of red rock, the isolated lava plug of a miniature and now totally eroded volcano. It is called Fischer's Column after Dr. Gustav Fischer, the German explorer who discovered Hell's Gate. At its base is a jumble of boulders.

There was a sudden scampering movement in this jumble, and I saw why the Verreaux's eagles are attracted to these particular cliffs— among the few places in this part of the Rift where they nest and breed.

A Wealth of Life

The base of the pinnacle was crawling with rock hyrax, or dassies, a favourite prey of the eagle. These

AN AUGUR BUZZARD ABOUT TO STRIKE

CLIFF ENTRANCE OF HELL'S GATE

concernedly sunning themselves.

But when the long, thin shadow of a bird of prey flicked across the grass, an old male dassie gave a high-pitched, mewing alarm call. One or two other dassies darted in alarm up the steep rock pile on feet equipped with rubber-like pads. In fact the sentinel need not have worried. For he had seen the silhouette of one of the lammergeiers, or bearded vultures, that nest in the cliffs above. A bird with narrow wings and a slender body ending in a wedge-shaped tail, the lammergeier exhibits interest in dassies only after they are dead, for it feeds on carrion.

Half a mile beyond the lonely pinnacle, the eastern wall of the gorge starts to close in. It, too, is a fault scarp, but a small one compared with the towering rock face opposite. Though Longonot was now hid-

mammals were almost certainly the "conies" described in the Old Testament. They are about the size of rabbits, and although coney is an old English word for rabbit, rabbits these creatures most definitely are not. With their short, pointed snouts and small ears, they look more like marmots. In fact the dassie, like the secretary bird, is unique. It has a special order, the Hyracoidea, all to itself, and its nearest living relative is, amazingly, the elephant.

Although dassies are preyed upon by leopards, servals, jackals and wild dogs as well as eagles, they can be surprisingly confiding with human beings. I stood dead still, and within minutes a dozen were un-

FISCHER'S COLUMN, A VOLCANIC PLUG

LAMMERGEIER NESTING RIDGE

EASTERN WALL OF THE GORGE

EMBARTA—THE HORSE

den behind the eastern wall, its work was plain to see. Much of its lava long ago streamed in the direction of Hell's Gate and overlies the earlier faulting of the scarps. Its volcanic ash is laid down in grey bands of slightly differing colours, each layer telling the story of a period of prolonged activity. Some strata are only inches thick, others three feet; the latter recording the times when Longonot was in full and lengthy eruption. The outcroppings of ash have a more rounded appearance than the rocks and lava, for centuries of torrential Rift Valley storms have softened their grey old faces.

Five miles from my starting point, the high country was becoming wilder and more barren, as were the twisting rock walls. Here, as the trail climbed, the whistling thorn trees grew taller in the dark volcanic soil. A cathedral tower of rock that the Masai tribesmen long ago named Embarta, the horse, rises from the gorge bottom. It is capped with a diminutive acacia whose wind-blown seed somehow once took root there. No matter how inaccessible or apparently hostile the environment, there are always plants that find a hold in the fertile volcanic soil.

Up to this point, the gorge was largely formed by rifting and by volcanic action. But now I reached a deep ravine cut by the action of water. From here, Naivasha's overflow must have rushed southwards with tempestuous force. There was water in the ravine's bottom now, red as blood with silt washed down by recent rains.

The last half mile of rapidly narrowing savannah yielded a bonus in terms of mammals. Six impala—a buck with lovely lyre-shaped horns and five hornless females—were munching their way towards me. Where grass gave way to thorn scrub on rising ground beneath the gorge wall, something yellowish-brown and as tall as a horse moved majestically through the red oat pastures. It was an eland, the largest of all antelope. If it were not for its long, straight, back-raked horns, the great beast, with its heavy dewlap, might easily be mistaken for a wild ox. In motion however, there is no mistaking it; even a big male of 1,000 pounds is as agile as a mustang. The

YOUNG BABOON GROOMING AN ELDER

SUCCULENT ON VOLCANIC ROCK

most bovine characteristics about it are that it provides great steaks—as all hunters will confirm—and it tames in captivity remarkably easily.

A troop of baboons moved through the grass, arranged for defence as formally as a military convoy. Young, adventurous males scouted the territory ahead, while the older dominant ones stayed in the centre with females and young. If the "scouts" sounded the alarm, then the females and young would retreat and the imposing old males move up to make a barrier of fangs in front of the weaker members of the troop. This group was in a peaceful mood, for they stopped and the younger members groomed their elders' fur, picking out snags and dirt. Mutual grooming

plays an important part in baboon society. It strengthens the bonds between individuals and establishes their place in the hierarchy.

Amidst the thorn scrub grew low green solanum bushes, carrying the small fruit called Sodom, or buck, apples, and where the earth was still moist from recent rains, a cluster of butterflies—African whites,

SODOM APPLES

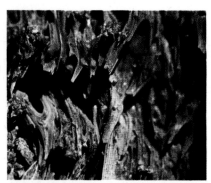

FLOW-PATTERN ON LAVA

A BUTTERFLY DRINKING

swallowtails and charaxes—uncurled their probosces to probe for droplets that would provide a drink.

The scene now began to have more than a touch of the satanic about it. Were the track plunging down instead of climbing steeply along the gorge's western shoulder, it would indeed have made a suitable entrance to Hades. Rounding a turn in an ash-layered cliff, I was faced with a jumble of debris that might have been Vulcan's personal slag-heap. The path was pushed to the lip of a ravine by a bullying shoulder of lava —pale grey and reddish drippings that still seemed so plastic in form they might have oozed and glowed

only yesterday. The place where the flow stops is littered with lumps of a black, shiny substance. This is obsidian, glass fused by immense volcanic heat, so brittle that African hunters once fashioned razor-sharp spear and arrow heads from it. Primitive tools chipped from Hell's Gate obsidian have been found as far away as the Serengeti plain, 200 miles south, in Tanzania.

This great bank of black, broken lava, which was to keep me company to the crest of Hell's Gate, still two miles away, welled out of a fissure created by the Rift's complex sinkings and crackings. Its lack of weathering showed that it was of recent origin—another sign that the subterranean forces that created the valley have not yet finished altering the face of Africa.

The top of the pass was visible now, though still distressingly high

above the obsidian pile. My target was a line of wavering puffs of white—puzzlingly transient, pale clouds rising like Indian smoke signals from the distant skyline. And already, with some hundreds of feet yet to climb, I was thirsty. But over many walks in Africa, I had taught myself not to drink until the last supportable moment. This is not masochism, but common sense. One sip always seems to demand another, and the water-bottle may have to last longer than planned.

At this height, I was not expecting to see much more wildlife, but Africa is never short of surprises. From beneath a high, red earth bank came a sharp nasal chorus of cries, as more than 100 birds fired themselves out of as many holes like gleaming missiles leaving their silos. Square-tailed, with vivid red chests beneath their white chin-stripes,

OBSIDIAN, BLACK VOLCANIC GLASS

they were white-fronted bee-eaters.

Some settled on trailing roots washed out of the bank. Others darted to a ravine nearby that held water from a recent storm. It was now a breeding ground for insects and the bee-eaters were feasting. They catch the insects in mid-air with their long, down-curved beaks, which are not only precise but sharp and strong—the tools they use to excavate the nesting and roosting holes that run deep into the bank.

The rains that filled the bee-eaters' ravine had also washed out the track ahead, carving deep, yawning gullies and cutting away volcanic ash. Only the week before, the pathway had been reported intact. The immense power of water to modify the friable African soil, once the top cover of grass and scrub has been removed, could not have been more clearly demonstrated.

ERODED VOLCANIC ASH

But the rain had done wildlife a good turn. Although the top of the pass offered nothing more tempting than barren acacia and thorn scrub, small V-shaped spoor imprinted in damp mud, now preserved as it dried, showed that dik-dik had been drinking here. There were also the spoor of baboon and leopard, and antelope droppings on the path.

One of these droppings was bowling along as if powered by a tiny motor. The motor was actually a dung-beetle many times smaller than its burden. As it scuttled the ball of dung backwards—using its hind legs, with its front legs on the ground—its progress was momen-

WHITE-FRONTED BEE-EATER

BEE-EATERS' NESTING HOLES

tarily thwarted by a tree root. With a gargantuan effort, it mounted the obstacle and continued its search for a spot where it could bury the dung and lay its eggs inside the ball. When the eggs hatched, the grubs would feed on the dropping.

The cratered peak of Longonot was now well-risen above the eastern wall of Hell's Gate. Although Longonot played a major part in creating the geological formations in

DISSOTIS FLOWERS IN A STEAM VENT

this gorge, it is nevertheless young in terms of the entire Rift Valley story. A friend who flew over the volcano recently saw a steam vent inside the scrub-filled, perfectly rounded crater. Any mountain that still looks like a volcano is most certainly a newcomer here. The older volcanoes that were present when the major faulting of the valley began have long since been worn down, or have collapsed into gigantic, open, shallow calderas. Longonot still lords it over Hell's Gate, even though its rim, too, has been partially eroded and lacks the perfectly symmetrical pattern expected in volcanoes that are, geologically speaking, still infants.

The white puffs of smoke signals

on the crest were nearer and much clearer now. As I worked my way towards them, I found that the pass had saved its biggest wildlife surprise for the last uphill mile. Beyond the jumble of obsidian rose a stand of flat-topped acacias—an ideal but, in the setting, unlikely browsing ground for giraffe. Then, to my amazement, a half-grown giraffe did indeed strut across the track. Another youngster and two adults followed. Immediately, they all began to lasso the topmost acacia branches with their long, velvety tongues. It always astonishes me that those delicate tongues can work their way through shoots and branches guarded by two-inch thorns.

The Objective Achieved

Now I began to scramble up the great bank of lava. I was panting and my mouth was parched. But, at last, after a scratching progress up an acacia-guarded citadel, I reached my objective.

The ground rumbled and hissed all around. Even through rubber soles, it was hot to the feet. There was a distinct smell of fire and brimstone, a most appropriate atmosphere to breathe at the very lintel of Hell's Gate. What had looked like smoke from two miles distant was revealed as steam, bubbling furiously from a hundred tiny fissures. Incredibly, pale lavender dissotis flowers grew here, watered by the condensing vapour. And through the steam-clouds loomed Longonot, guardian of Hell's Gate and Naivasha, both of which it helped create from the red-hot vitals of the Rift.

AT THE CREST OF THE GATE, A LAVA FLOW FLANKING LONGONOT

4/ Cauldrons of Soda

*The whole deposit looks exactly like a lake which has been
frozen over with snow-ice all the winter and is breaking up
and partly flooded by the thaw in the spring.*

A. M. HARRISON/ REPORT TO THE EAST AFRICA SYNDICATE

To the south of Lake Naivasha, in the 140-mile stretch between the two
large volcanoes, Longonot and Ol Doinyo Lengai, lies perhaps the most
awful region of the Rift. The southern end of the trough between the two
mountains holds what to my mind are the world's most inhospitable
lakes, Magadi and Natron—two corrosive sumps of water and soda. At
first sight it seems incredible that anything could live on or near the
lakes' scum of sodium carbonate. Considering the conditions, there is a
surprising amount of wildlife at both; in Magadi, there are fish that man-
age to live in the extreme environment provided by hot springs at the
lake's south end; there are birds that live off the few fresh-water springs;
and Natron is the breeding ground for almost all of East Africa's flamingo
population—a fact kept secret by its caustic flats until the early 1950s.

The route along which I drove southwards from Naivasha to the soda
lakes at first winds up from the floor of the Rift, climbing the eastern, or
Kikuyu, scarp. Near the top it passes close to a spot notable, not only for
its beauty, but also for its place in the Rift's history. It was near here that
J. W. Gregory gazed into the formation that was eventually to bear his
name, glimpsing "the plain, with its patches of green swamp and glittering sand and, far to the west, the long, dull grey scarp of the plateau
which forms the western boundary of the valley". The nearly vertical
walls, the thick bush just beyond the roadside, and the toylike appearance of tracks 2,000 feet below brought home to me vividly what it must

have been like for a heavily-loaded safari to climb down on foot. No matter how many times I travel this road, or how often I visit the Rift's remoter wilderness areas, I never fail to catch my breath at this prospect.

Some 30 miles further on are the Ngong Hills. Like almost all other mountains in the Rift, their origin is volcanic, and they stand in a series of peaks, their green summits rounded and softened by erosion, with all sign of their original craters worn away. Many people unfamiliar with East Africa imagine it to be a seer land, burned red and yellow, but its hills, at least, are always green.

It is hard to imagine anything much wilder—granted that I was travelling a road of sorts—than the 50-mile journey from the Ngong Hills to Magadi. As I started my descent, a man strode over the green crest to my left, wearing a red ochre robe and carrying a tall, broad-pointed spear. His hair was tied in small knots and shone with grease. I had entered Masai tribal territory, and this man, herding his cattle, was a Masai *moran*, or warrior. The plains and scrub that stretched out ahead, far down the Rift and over the Crater Highlands of Tanzania towards the Serengeti, were all his on which to graze his cattle.

On either side rose scarps of basalt, some of them 50 feet, others 100 feet or more, in height—the results of faulting within the greater fault of the main valley itself. The scarps leant against each other, like a shelf of books that had collapsed sideways. Acacias, hung with the coconut-like nests of weaver birds, dotted the countryside. Small herds of dainty, fawn Thomson's and Grant's gazelles broke cover, trotted away flicking their tails, and then stopped briefly to cast glances backwards over their shoulders. Parties of baboons crossed the path, organized for maximum protection with the older males flanking the females, which carried babies at their breasts and the larger children on their backs, jockey-fashion.

Twenty miles from Lake Magadi, the country became softer and greener where a stream, partly dried out, ran down from the scarps. More Grant's and Thomson's gazelles were grazing there, and a blossom of white in the valley bottom revealed itself on closer viewing as hundreds of European storks, searching for grasshoppers and other insects to sustain them on the long, northward migration up the Rift, over the Red Sea, through the Jordan Valley, and on to nest in Eastern Europe and Russia.

A final dusty descent beside yet another fault scarp and at last Magadi was in sight, a monstrous growth of pure soda. Lake Magadi has a weird fascination all of its own. Its predominant colour is an unearthly pink, reminiscent of some decaying confectionery, like coconut icing. Close to the edges, where minor fault scarps rise abruptly, the thin scum of water mirrors the greens, greys and sombre browns of the rocks. In certain evening and early morning lights, the surface achieves a rare beauty. At sunset I have seen its soda flats transmuted into purest gold. But in the uncompromising, overpowering heat and light of midday, Magadi is a shimmering hellscape.

There are other alkaline lakes of the Rift, of course, but with the exception of nearby Natron, they are far milder. These others are sodary because they lack an outlet for the minerals that flow into them in solution from the rivers and streams draining the surrounding country, which is rich in chemicals from volcanic ash. But Magadi's soda apparently surges up thick and caustic from the thermal intestines of the Rift. There is no other way to account for the fact that the Magadi Soda Company has been digging, dredging and sucking the native soda out since the early 1900s without making the slightest impression on the lake. All the evidence suggests that Lake Magadi is actually gaining on the miners.

No one can say precisely how Magadi performs this miracle. It seems certain that the springs that feed it well up into its bed through layers of pure soda. Even so, the source of the subterranean water is a mystery. In one sense, it might not have to flow in from anywhere: there are vast reservoirs of water stored in many places beneath the earth's surface. Perhaps a lake lies undiscovered beneath Magadi, its waters seeping upwards under pressure. One possible theory is that the hidden outflow from Naivasha might seep in this direction. The drop in elevation between the two lakes—some 5,000 feet—is certainly in favour of the theory and there is much porous lava buried in the Rift floor between them.

I drove through a settlement where freshly extracted soda dries in piles of pink crystals. The track climbs a dusty rise to a police post. Here I was required to report and write my time of arrival and destination. It was impressed on me that it was even more important that I sign out on my return. Once I had driven beyond the last worker's bungalow, only a land of hostile nothingness lay ahead of me. A Kikuyu policeman asked me what time I expected to be back from the hot springs at the south end of the lake. If I disappeared, there would at least be a record of my schedule. The country between Magadi and Natron is not an area to venture into without plenty of petrol and water.

I drove through the scrub as close to the lake's edge as I could get. Far away towards the northern end a dark spot dancing in a mirage, was, I knew, the Soda Company's dredger, sucking up the hell's brew of the lake.

As I drove southward, I came across a few flamingoes and several other species of birds, living close to the hot springs that supply some fresh water to this end of the lake. A mixture of long-billed, probing waders—reeves mainly and some little stints—wandered round the margins, while a party of African spoonbills swept methodically for crustacea with their ladle-like beaks. At one point, as I veered briefly away from the shore, thick lava dust suddenly whirled up as a pair of eland—antelope as large as oxen—burst out of the thorn scrub, easily outstripping my mere 20-miles-an-hour progress.

Where the lake ended, two arms of greyish mud ran up into the bush. The mud looked solid enough, even though it was overlaid in places with a skin of water. But I had no wish to crash through into what could prove to be stinking black ooze below. I inched forward in four-wheel drive and discovered that the softness was all on top. Extremely relieved, I felt firm ground under my wheels again and tackled the next tongue of the flats with more confidence, emerging on a wide soda lagoon that made that minor moment of tension quite worthwhile. The flats were alive with game, although the stupefying heat on the sodary mud distorted vision. Even at a mere two or three hundred yards' range, lines of zebra were transformed into legless, dancing blobs that melted and re-formed as they moved sedately across the grey horizon. Something alarmed a party of Thomson's gazelles and they galloped away, splashing up the water under their hooves. It was so hot that I almost expected to see water turn to steam as it struck the ground beside the rill from which they had disturbed it.

At last I reached the hot springs themselves and began to search for the fish I had come to see. They were *Tilapia grahami*, a dwarf species— only two or three inches long—of a very common African family. They survive, feeding on green algae that grows in the springs, in conditions of alkalinity and heat that would kill other fish. The water in which they live is almost too hot for the human hand to bear in comfort, but there are limits to the endurance of even these robust creatures. This frontier was clearly delineated: much of the bottom and sides of the springs was covered with light green algae on which the fish feed, but close to the places where the water gushed up near boiling point from the rock below, the algae suddenly became a darker green. At this point, the temperature became too high for the fish to bear and the potential source of food had remained uneaten. Unlike many animals that live in extreme conditions, however, this remarkable fish is not over-specialized to the point of vulnerability; it can tolerate great changes in its habitat. When the rains come, its pools are diluted and their temperature drops, but the *grahami* remain healthy and active.

Walking back to the Land Rover, I took a final glance across the soda flats. They were impressive, certainly, yet I had the feeling that if I were stranded on them I would have a fair chance of walking off. The lake is comparatively narrow and the soda for the most part appears reasonably solid. It will never fill me with the state of near terror generated by its awesome neighbour, Lake Natron, 20 miles south.

While *magadi* means "soda lake" in Masai, natron is the chemical word for natural sodium carbonate. Although Lake Natron is thought to be less productive of soda than Magadi, it is considerably larger—a gigantic bath, part-liquid, part-soda, ten miles wide by 40 miles long. Such a volume of crude soda must surely be delivered to the lake, as at Magadi, from underground concentrations rather than by run-off from the surrounding countryside.

To explore Natron from the ground calls for a minor expedition. For my own inspection of the lake, I decided to fly. But even this form of transport entails an element of risk, for a combination of scenery, colour and heat haze distorts a pilot's sense of level flight. My pilot, the wildlife film-maker, Alan Root, usually delighted in showing me game and scenery from a height of around 30 feet. But as we flew over Natron, he gave the surface at least 100 feet clearance, and kept a wary eye on the rate-of-climb indicator to ensure he was not descending. An unintended descent into that dreadful place hardly bears thinking about. I would hope to die immediately in such a crash, rather than perish lingeringly of heat stroke and dehydration as caustic salts flayed the skin from my body.

Natron's ability to deceive the eye derives from the area's peculiar combination of geography, chemical consistency and climate. Natron is a typical long, narrow, fjord-like Rift lake, flanked to the west by the towering wall of the Nguruman escarpment; to the north-east and south-east lie two extinct volcanoes, Shombole and Gelai. Dead centre at the south end of Natron rises the most impressive volcano of all, the still-active Ol Doinyo Lengai, the Masai's "Mountain of God".

The mountains are just one element in the spell Natron casts on air travellers; another is the character of Natron's surface. Like Magadi it is a mass of ghastly pink blotches caused by the algal growth that thrives in the otherwise deadly soda. Natron is sheltered by escarpment and volcanoes, and thus is frequently glassily calm, a perfect reflecting

Although only a few large animals populate the margins of the soda lakes, a host of hardy insects hunt along their formidable, volcanic shores. Scavengers like the mole cricket (bottom right) find a wealth of animal and vegetable rubbish to eat; earwigs even eat their own kind (far right). The toughest creatures, however, have their limits, as the picture of the dragonfly shows (top right). Overcome by heat and fumes during its low-level aerial hunting, this predatory insect has drowned in the hot, bitter waters of a soda spring.

DROWNED DRAGONFLY

CANNIBAL EARWIG

MOLE CRICKET

surface. Combined reflected images of green hills, grey rock, blue sky, all caught in its pink mirror surface, produce visual confusion enough. Add to this heat haze and mirage from a surface whose mid-day temperature often reaches 150 degrees Fahrenheit, and it is impossible to tell where lake ends and shore begins. Lengai, rising at the end of the lake, performs this double game most bewilderingly of all.

Far more experienced and adept fliers than the human pilots of light aircraft crash, to their short-lived surprise, into the waters of Natron. The ends of the lake at migration time are littered with the corpses of birds that have made precisely the navigational error of which Alan Root was aware. Deceived by topography and reflection, they descend when intending to fly straight and level. Many of the birds apparently make their fatal mistake when migrating at night. It is not hard to imagine how, in conditions of moonlight or bright African starlight, the visual disorientation can be disastrous.

Despite Natron's terrifying nature, flying over the lake on a fine, still, early morning can be one of the most sublime experiences in Africa. From two or three thousand feet, I have looked down not only on a wine-pink lake but on Shombole, Gelai and Lengai and, beyond them to the east and west, even greater volcanoes of the past. In clear conditions, Mount Meru and Kilimanjaro show up eastwards. To the south-west, the huge green massif of the Crater Highlands rises beyond Lengai.

At low altitude, even in the aircraft, I could feel the oven heat beating upwards off the soda flats. At ground level, on the lake shore, it must be like standing on the oven top itself, hotter yet than Magadi. The familiar, acrid smell of soda flooded thick inside the cockpit as we slid the canopy back for a better view. With flaps lowered, our light aircraft could fly safely at 50 miles per hour and it was possible at this speed to make out every detail. We flew slowly down the eastern shore. Where a river, the Uaso Nyiro, flows in, there is a wide expanse of fresher water. Fifteen miles down the lake, a rough track connecting Natron with Magadi comes in. It was built to serve a now derelict magnesite mine. But for this very basic track the lake would still not be accessible even to most four-wheel-drive vehicles.

From the air, game trails and the animals that made them showed up clearly. I saw zebra, oryx—large antelope whose long straight horns are said to have given rise to the legend of the unicorn—and awkward-looking, shaggy wildebeeste. An ostrich had ventured out on the firm white soda bordering the shore, thought better of it and wisely turned back. One thermal spring, marked by a steam vent, was surrounded by the prints of many game animals, including rhinoceros and lion.

Alan pointed down to a single large acacia. It had been from here, he shouted, that naturalist Leslie Brown had set out to find the breeding grounds of the Rift Valley flamingoes, and had walked alone across the Natron soda flats in an extraordinary journey. He made it back alive— though only just—to complete what is possibly the greatest epic of the Rift since the early explorers first entered the Valley.

The nesting grounds of the Rift's 3,000,000 flamingoes had long been a mystery. The Masai around Lake Natron had their own explanation. From time to time they saw fully-fledged young birds, still in their grey, juvenile plumage, standing in the shallows on the edge of the lake. They accounted for this by saying that the birds were hatched out of the lake itself and simply walked ashore when they were ready to fly. Who can blame them for thinking so? The world of Lake Natron is weird enough to make anything seem possible, even to scientists.

Leslie Brown, then chief agricultural officer for Kenya, was the first to employ an aircraft in the search. He found what seemed from the air to be two large colonies several miles offshore on the Natron soda flats. However, the only way to be certain that flamingoes were breeding was to approach them on foot. He marked the acacia tree over which we now circled as the nearest point to the colonies from which to start walking.

Having risen at dawn and trudged the few miles from his own camp at the foot of Mount Gelai, Brown left the grudging shade of the lone acacia, equipped with only a canvas water bottle, and started out across the soda towards the colonies. At first, the going on the hard white soda close to the edge was comparatively good. Then he began to break through the crust into the thick, stinking, black ooze just below. Leslie Brown is immensely strong and, as a wildfowler brought up on Scottish estuaries, he understands the mechanics of walking on mud. But no estuary mud ever matched this. Beyond the hard stuff, a half-mile of shallow water waited. This was where he quite rightly expected trouble. A scum of pinkish water littered with the bodies of dead locusts overlay softer soda. As the water gradually deepened, the soda became mushier until his feet sank into foul-smelling sulphurous mud beneath.

Now every step in that intense heat dragged energy out of his body. He struggled across the shallows, confidently expecting to walk the rest of the way to the colony on the hard white floes he could see ahead. Here, the soda had formed itself into polygonal plates with raised edges, looking like giant water lily leaves. The soda lilies were, in fact, brittle

in the extreme. He was soon crashing through and floundering about
once again. The mud below was drier but more glutinous and the effort
of extracting one gumboot often buried the other foot even deeper. At
one point he was on all fours but he dared not stop for fear of sinking
and becoming immoveably stuck. A further crisis followed: when he
drank from his canvas water bag he found the soda had impregnated it.
The water was bitter and made him retch, but he drank nearly all of it
before it could become any worse.

When he finally gave up his attempt to reach the colony, he had few
reserves of strength left for the return journey. He later recalled his
journey back: "Then began a frightful treadmill. Crushed by disappointment, and far more exhausted than I knew, I had to make my way back
across the two hundred yards of sticky mud before I could reach the
shallow water where conditions would be easier. The full weight of my
fatigue seemed suddenly to strike me like a blow and I realised for the
first time that I would be extremely lucky to escape alive. I had reached
the little soda island only by putting out all the effort of which I was
capable, driven by the spur of enthusiasm. Now I must cover the same
ground starting from extreme exhaustion, in the hottest hours of the
day, and without any spare water. I knew that I could succeed only if I
husbanded carefully the last remnants of my strength. And so I set out,
but the mud forced me to continuous racking effort. I found I could take
five or six steps before I was brought up short, plunging in the filth and
gasping for breath. At each halt I could only allow myself a momentary
respite, for I sank slowly into the black foul mud beneath the crust,
and I dared not sink too far for fear that I would be unable to wrench
my boots free again.

"So it went on—five or six steps, reeling with exhaustion and barely
able to see in front of me, so that I even lost the clear black trail of my
outward passage and could think only of steering generally towards
the bulk of Gelai. And this was just as well, for by some strange
quirk of fortune I struck a slightly easier patch of going where, once,
I actually made about ten yards between halts, treading delicately
along the raised crust of a soda ridge. So great was the relief at this
break in my enforced rhythm of struggle that it seemed as if Providence
was lifting me bodily and helping me through.

"If I had not been a strong man and an experienced mud-walker I
should be there yet, the flesh dissolved from my bones and the skeleton
stuck in the mud. It was partly the thought of the beastliness of this way
of dying, and partly anger at my own stupidity, that kept me going.

Suffice it now to say that after two hundred yards or so of appalling struggle I found the mud growing wetter. I knew then that the worst was over, that I was coming to the part overlaid by water and that I should escape."

When Brown at last reached hard, white crust again, he took off his gumboots, which were filled with crystalline soda, to find his legs raw with red blisters that turned black in the air as he watched them. He was still faced with a seven-mile walk back along the shore to his camp and the 45-mile drive back to Magadi. He lay more or less unconscious for three days in the Magadi Soda Company's hospital and spent a further week swathed in bandages. The legs took six weeks to recover and finally had to be repaired by skin grafts.

In 1957, Leslie Brown assaulted Natron again, and this time reached a colony of breeding flamingoes by walking over comparatively firm brown mud at the Gelai end. But then he vowed never to set foot on the lake's dreadful surface again.

He confesses that he was always nervous when flying across Natron. I certainly was. At one hundred feet, should the engine fail, there is simply nowhere to go, except in. Even as I looked down on the strange pink whorls of soda on Natron's port-wine surface, I was listening tensely to the engine's beat. Alan banked the plane away at last. We set course towards the western Rift wall, the Nguruman Escarpment, climbing the first heavily treed step and then pulling up sharply to clear the final scarp. We banked and looked down into dense green gullies. Natron was far away below, pink, beautiful and enticing once more.

Caustic Swamps and Bitter Waters

Through the aeons of the Rift's shiftings, the history of the lakes that formed in many of the valley's troughs and depressions has been as troubled as that of the land that created them. Rivers feeding and draining the lakes have changed course or disappeared and the chemicals in the land around them have been renewed with every eruption of lava and ash from beneath the earth's crust. As a result, many of the lakes that originally held fresh water have been spoiled by the intrusion of mineral salts, washed in by rain from volcanic slopes or welling up from springs. The most abundant of these is a water-soluble alkali: sodium carbonate, known as soda.

The soda affects the lakes in two ways, making some bitter but drinkable and encrusting others with thick beds of nearly pure alkali, so that any water that accumulates on top is reduced to an acrid, poisonous film. The outcome depends on the nature of the water supply and on whether or not the lake has an outlet. An outflowing river bears soda away, but in the absence of an outlet, water is lost only by evaporation, which leaves the soda to concentrate until it dries out completely.

The lakes that lie in the deepest, hottest trough in the Central Rift—Magadi and Natron—are the Rift's greatest tracts of soda. They lack outlets and nearly all the water that reaches them is already very alkaline: much of the run-off from the surrounding hills passes through the effluvium of Ol Doinyo Lengai, an active volcano so rich in alkali that even its crust is white. The springs nearby contain up to two per cent in solution and soda surging from below pockmarks the lakes' margins.

Magadi and Natron are arid, caustic heat traps; only 16 inches of rain fall on them each year, but over the same period 130 inches of water evaporate. Under the circumstances, it is hardly surprising that they support little wildlife. Flamingoes that feed on soda algae are the only large animals fully adapted to these extreme conditions.

By contrast, Lake Rudolf supports a wide variety of fish and the birds that prey on them. Its shores partly consist of volcanoes, and soda does, therefore, enter it by run-off. However, fresh water from the river Omo dilutes the lake and so the soda does not become significantly concentrated by evaporation. Rudolf's waters thus remain within limits that allow life to flourish.

Cracking and buckling in the intense tropical heat, the soda flats of Lake Magadi surround a shallow puddle of alkali-saturated water.

A view northwards over Lake Natron in
the dry season reveals white "tide marks"
of crystallizing soda alternating with
dark ooze of the lake bed. During
rains the lake rises, but wherever the
water is shallow it becomes heated
by the sun and evaporates quickly to
leave ridges of soda. The lake is supplied
by alkaline springs below its surface and
by streams flowing over soda-rich soil,
like the one at the bottom right entering
from the direction of the volcano Gelai.

Swirls of hundreds of flamingoes appear white against the lurid surface of Lake Natron, stained red by the algae that thrive on soda.

White, soda-rimmed craters pock-mark the surface of Lake Natron where bubbles of liquid or gas have burst upwards through its crust.

Along the south shore of Lake Rudolf, the extinct cones of Nabuyatom (foreground) and Abili Agituk jut out into the water, which they have helped contaminate with soda. Although the lake is bitter, it supports many forms of life, particularly an immense bloom of algae that changes the colour of Rudolf from sky blue to jade green according to the amounts of sunlight and wind.

Snaking into the middle of Lake Rudolf, the fresh-water river Omo flows towards the camera between its own raised banks, or levées. These and the bird's-foot delta in the foreground are accumulations of debris and silt, carried out into Rudolf by the fresh river water, which is comparatively light and therefore flows over the top of the denser soda solution already in the lake. The debris is deposited as the river current gradually slows down, and builds over the years into firm ground.

5/ Flamingoes by the Million

*Lesser flamingoes are rather remote beings
inhabiting a world only they can inhabit with enjoyment.*

LESLIE BROWN/ *THE MYSTERY OF THE FLAMINGOES*

Imagine a river of flame fifty yards wide and three miles long. From it rises a continual grumbling, growling murmur. As I approached across the powdery grey soda flats along the shore of Lake Nakuru, 100 miles northwest of Nairobi, the growl increased to a roar. I saw flames in the carpet of fire flickering in uneasy movement. As if my approach were fanning the conflagration, the wave of red curved suddenly outward into the lake. A few yards closer to the water's edge and the pattern broke up into individual tongues of fire.

Each flicker was a flamingo running in panic to take off. At this moment, the flamingo was grotesque, a creature out of *Alice*, a suitable butt for Tenniel's pen. The webbed feet stamped the surface to foam as the scarlet wings beat for lift. Such an alarm, raised by human intrusion, is sometimes purely a local one. But often it proves infectious, so that the ripple runs at least part way through an immense throng of birds, stretching as far as the eye can see along the water's edge. Ten thousand flame-pink birds may suddenly be poured into the blue bowl of the sky.

Though the take-off is anything but graceful, after only a dozen paces a miraculous transformation takes place. Each bird, so clumsy in earth-bound motion, has become, in flight—and it is impossible not to reach for some technically aerodynamic comparisons—a miniature jet aeroplane. The comparison is not an exact one. The wings of a supersonic jet are set back towards the tail. The flamingo's wings are mid-set, perfectly and equally dividing trailing legs from reaching head and neck. In front of the wings, the image of a streamlined super-jet is more exact. Even the heavy, downpointed bill bears its resemblance to the aircraft's nose, lowered for a landing.

Whatever else lives and breathes throughout the length and breadth of the Rift Valley, the greatest faunal success story belongs to the flamingo. There are about five million flamingoes, belonging to six different species, in the entire world. Of these, at least three million live on the lakes of the Rift. There are only two species in this vast gathering and their names exactly fit their physical appearances—the greater and the lesser flamingo. Apart from differences in plumage and beak they appear similar in formation and colouring, but they represent the extreme ends of the size scale of the flamingo family, one standing almost six feet tall, the other being about half that height. The four intermediate species all come from the New World. Of the three million African birds, perhaps 50,000 are greaters, the rest lessers. They range the length of the Rift, wherever there are sodary lakes. I have seen them in huge numbers all the way from the Danakil Depression in Ethiopia to Lakes Manyara and Eyasi in Tanzania. Despite their wanderings, there is only one place in the Rift that can be considered their true home—Lake Nakuru. On this one small lake, barely four miles by six, it is often possible to see more than two million flame-pink birds.

Nakuru has been called the greatest bird spectacle in the world. It well deserves its title. Most of its shore was gazetted a National Park by the Kenya Government in 1961, the remainder in 1968. The Park is a narrow strip varying between a mile and a few hundred yards wide that runs beside the lake for most of its circumference. Joined to it is the Baharini Sanctuary, a lovely area of shoreline and acacia woodland that was once the farm of John Hopcroft, a young Kenyan who has dedicated his land and his entire efforts to the study and protection of Lake Nakuru and its birds.

What draws flamingoes in such huge numbers to Nakuru is food: diatoms, the blue-green algae *Spirulina*, in incredible concentrations that also support populations of brine shrimps and other small crustaceans. The soda-saturated water produces this rich food supply faster than all the flamingoes and other water birds can extract it, at an estimated rate of at least 200 tons per day. One reason for this abundance is the chemicals in the water. The other is the lake's location. The algae, like all green plants, need sunlight. Nakuru is set close to the Equator, at 5,767 feet, where year-round it is bathed in the ultraviolet rays comparatively unfiltered at high altitudes and beneficial to plant growth. The source of food, consequently, is there for the getting.

The snag is that while the vegetables in the broth are nourishing in the extreme, the liquid of the soda soup itself is lethal to the birds. But the evolution of a sophisticated pumping and straining process has ensured that the flamingo hordes have no need to drink the broth to get the vegetables (when they need water, they drink from fresh springs around the soda lakes). In ecological terms they have found themselves a niche that no other animal occupies. Their success is measured by the size of their population.

How the flamingoes take advantage of the food in a toxic soda soup can be seen by closely watching a batch of lessers feeding just offshore. The lesser's bill, a dark carmine red that looks almost black except at the tip, provides the specialized tool needed. Internally the flattened surfaces of both upper and lower bills are covered with fine hairs, lamellae, which interlock to form a sieve when the bill is closed. This strainer can retain particles as small as 1/1250 inch. In addition a line of bristles along the bill opening prevents pieces of food larger than 1/50 inch from reaching the sieve itself. The feeding birds suspend this ungainly, but superbly efficient, apparatus upside down in the water. The bill is submerged almost to the nostrils. What happens then cannot be seen from shore: the water is sucked in and out of the closed bill as if by a pump, the piston being the bird's tongue, moving up and down inside the closed beak.

While the vegetarian lesser flamingoes pump algae from the lake, the greater flamingoes feed on the crustaceans in much the same way. They use a rather coarser strainer, consisting of bony plates rather than filter hairs inside the beak. Quite often greater flamingoes employ an additional technique of their own to extract food from the mud, paddling in the silt to dislodge the minute forms of life embedded in it.

The detailed techniques of flamingoes' feeding methods are difficult to observe, but some other characteristics are spectacularly obvious. Probably the most striking of all flamingo acts is their massed courtship display, which sometimes continues for weeks or even months on end. The behaviour—indeed the whole question of flamingo breeding—is mysterious. They often display, but they do not necessarily follow through and nest, for they do not breed every year.

Whatever starts this behaviour off, once begun, it rapidly gathers momentum until suddenly there are thousands of birds displaying in the

A catastrophe that overtook flamingoes in 1962 is documented in these two pictures. The lesser flamingoes, which usually breed in the soda shallows of Lake Natron, were driven by floods to the soda-saturated Lake Magadi, nearby. Just when the eggs were about to hatch, Magadi's shallows became too dry and many birds deserted their nests (top). Chicks that did hatch became encrusted with soda anklets (bottom), and although wildlife field workers helped to free some 10,000 of them, thousands more died.

midst of thousands more who appear totally unconcerned. Probably most of the disinterested ones are not yet ripe for mating. Some experts say that flamingoes are not sexually mature until they are seven years old.

The ritual is an unbelievably noisy one. The displaying birds parade up and down, jammed closely together; heads raised and stiff-necked, they march and countermarch in a continuously moving column. In Leslie Brown's words: "The whole looks like some strange composite monster with a thousand legs, with the legs and the necks moving rapidly all the time, while the bodies remain at one level and seem to float along in a block." Sometimes individuals stop to fluff out their feathers and then suddenly drop their heads as if their necks have been broken. Some, on the outside of the displaying group, suddenly stand bolt upright and shoot out their wings. And then the clamorous, weirdly intricate tribal dance continues.

The actual breeding does not occur on Nakuru. Though the courting is done here, and nests are often built here and on other lakes, the flamingoes invariably abandon them and, for reasons not yet understood, resort to Lake Natron, 150 miles to the south, to mate and lay eggs.

It was here that Leslie Brown observed something over half a million pairs at their nests. These they build by squirting or ladelling wet mud into a volcano shape, which then dries and hardens in the sun. These nests are built far out on the mud and soda flats of Natron, and are peculiarly subject to disasters. In November and December of 1957, for instance, Brown recorded that 200,000 nests were washed out by rising water. And in 1962, the whole flamingo population of East Africa was threatened by a catastrophe of huge proportions.

Drought followed by floods in Natron had so oppressed the flamingoes of the Rift that they were forced, for the first time in memory, to try to nest on the forbidding soda flats of Lake Magadi. But the concentration of soda in Magadi proved too much for the birds. Wildlife filmmaker Alan Root discovered that the youngest chicks, too small to move about much, were becoming trapped in deposits of pure soda that formed round their legs like lumps of concrete. Alan and his wife, Joan, began a rescue operation. With a few helpers, they broke away the chicks' soda anklets by hand, and, when this proved too slow, chipped them off with a light blow from a hammer. Soon the East African Wildlife Society, the World Wildlife Fund and even the British Army based in what was then Tanganyika sent money and reinforcements. At least 10,000 chicks were eventually saved by releasing them and by driving them into areas where the soda concentration was lower.

It may be tempting to suppose that the Rift's flamingoes had never before made the error of nesting on Lake Magadi, but this is very unlikely to be true. The same combination of drought and flood that had denied them their traditional nesting grounds on Natron for two seasons running must have occurred many times previously in the changing history of the Rift. As proof, a fossilized soda anklet was recently found similar to those worn by the young birds in the Magadi débâcle.

So stunning is the flamingo spectacle on Nakuru that it is easy to overlook the lake's other bird life. Four hundred species have been recorded around the lake, though none is as well adapted to the sodary environment as the flamingo. Fishing fleets of great white pelicans communally trawl for their living, drawn by the fish recently introduced into the lake as an anti-mosquito measure. (The fish are the same *Tilapia grahami* that have so successfully adapted to the hot springs of Magadi.) Neat little shoveler ducks swing their large spatulate bills, sweeping up the algae and trapping it in lamellae similar to those inside the flamingoes' beaks. Several species of waders bob and strut in their search for molluscs, insects and crustaceans. And marabou storks, that sometimes prey on flamingoes, parade ominously on the lake's shoreline.

If there is a bird of more evil omen than the marabou in the length of the Rift, I have yet to meet it. Not even the griffon or the hooded vulture approach the marabou in physical meanness of appearance. Long ago, someone—it must have been an Army officer—christened these great birds Adjutant storks. There is certainly something in their speculative, parading gait reminiscent of a critical Regimental Adjutant inspecting a parade. Even this comparison seems to take too kindly a view of the character concerned. To me it far more resembles the character of an undertaker, hands held behind back and obsequiously hidden in the tails of a rusty old frock coat.

This funereal image is certainly closer to the storks' wholetime occupation and pre-occupation, for they are not so much hunters as funeral directors and grave-robbers. Their main living is from the dead. In this they resemble vultures, but they have certain anatomical limitations. The marabou does not have the vulture's talons, nor its powerful, ripping, hooked beak. Yet the beak that nature has provided the stork with is powerful in quite a different way. It has the power of a pick-axe combined with the grasping ability of an outsize pair of long-nosed pliers. This means that, when tackling a large mammal carcase, the marabou has to wait for other scavengers to open up the corpse before it can probe and reach for the soft interior tit-bits. But the beak is also a formidable weapon with which to strike living prey. At Nakuru, young flamingoes sometimes provide the marabous with just such victims.

One day on the grey soda flats I watched predatory marabous in action. Dense parties of young flamingoes, perhaps six months old—pale, greyish, their immature plumage not affected by the carotene pigments in the algae that give the adults their soft pink colour—were grouped together in the water. Several marabous stalked about on the beach with an air of studied disinterest. Their pink throat pouches—whose purpose, by the way, no ornithologist has yet satisfactorily explained—wobbled obscenely. Suddenly one marabou took off and flew low and straight towards the flamingoes.

A marabou on the ground is both macabre and grotesque. It is, however, a magnificent and accomplished flier, able to soar with the best, while in level flight its ten-foot wing-span provides it with handsome acceleration. It was halfway to the flamingo group before they reacted. There was no time for those in the centre of the closely packed throng to take off. The birds began to stampede through the shallows. The marabou pressed on into the middle of the pack. It was as if the great stork had marked down one weak or injured bird and was determined to have this one alone. If this were true, then the marabou had remarkable eyesight to be able to detect its victim's failings in the first place, so dense was the assembly of flamingoes.

The end of the chase was near. Many of the flamingoes had at last succeeded in taking off. The marabou kept on and on, skimming down to run in for the kill through the lashed-up water. A few devastating blows with that pickaxe bill quickly finished the job. Those birds that escaped pitched a few hundred yards up the shore. And there another marabou strutted, perhaps awaiting its own opportunity for attack.

The Flamingoes' Sodary Home

The alkaline waters of the Great Rift Valley's soda lakes are fatal to most living creatures, yet in the shallows of many such lakes—especially Natron and Nakuru—millions of flamingoes can be seen apparently sipping the lethal broth.

The explanation is an unusual evolutionary adaptation that allows the flamingoes to get food from the soda solution without ingesting the corrosive liquid. There are two species of the birds: the lesser, which eats blue-green algae growing near the water surface, and the greater, standing head and neck taller, which sifts the bottom mud for tiny molluscs and crustaceans. Both depend for survival on their highly specialized bills, which are similar in design.

The flamingo bill is heavy and awkward-looking and bends abruptly downwards halfway along its length. The bird uses it like a ladle, feeding with its head upside down so that the "bowl" points in towards its legs. Opening the beak slightly, it sucks in water or mud by swaying its head from side to side and pumping with its tongue. A system of bristles on the inside of the beak excludes large, unrequired objects. A further network of finer bristles lies flat during this operation, but when the sodary liquid is expelled, the bristles are erected to trap the food particles, which can then be safely swallowed without the soda.

Both food supplies in the soda lakes contain canthaxanthin, a substance very similar chemically to Vitamin A, which turns the flamingoes pink. Away from the lakes they fade to white and in zoos they are fed synthetic canthaxanthin in order not to disappoint visitors. Strangely, pink is a colour often at odds with their surroundings, a contrast that might seem to make them easy prey for predators. But there are only a few predators of flamingoes, such as the marabou stork, and even it attacks only fledglings or weaklings.

The flamingoes take full advantage of their specialized niche. In the Rift, with its many soda lakes, there are more of them than in any other place on earth. In any one lake at any one time there may be two million flamingoes or more—mostly lesser flamingoes, which outnumber the greaters by as much as 200 to one. That number can remove up to 11,000 tons of algae from the water a month. The fast-growing algae can more than keep pace with this loss, and for the flamingoes the lakes remain an undiminished cornucopia.

Sleeping flamingoes stir with the early morning sun and begin to feed. Night and day they remain in the alkaline waters, their webbed feet supporting them on the soft mud. The lake acts both as their source of food and as a protection from most predators. An occasional fledgling may fall victim to a lance-billed marabou stork, but otherwise the only casualties in a flamingo colony are eggs or chicks in nests that can be reached over firm ground by enterprising, prowling animals such as hyenas or jackals.

In a breeding colony of greater flamingoes, the canopy of ruffled plumage and the forest of legs provide a secure home for the chicks.

A greater flamingo chick receives a parent's preening; soon it will be pushed out for a Spartan upbringing in adolescent colonies.

A great cloud of lesser flamingoes takes to the air (left), necks outstretched to counterbalance their long legs. Like many other waterfowl, they may well be unable to fly at all when they moult in the breeding season. Luckily, their breeding quarters are invariably on a soda lake, where there are few predators.

Gawky and vulnerable, lesser flamingoes run through the shallows (above) and beat their wings for take-off. It is a dangerous moment. A marabou stork that chooses its moment can easily intercept a weak one as it scrambles to escape into the air, knock it into the water and there peck it to death.

Mirrored in the lake, lesser flamingoes huddle in a tight group to prevent breezes disrupting the calm water that is ideal for feeding.

With their heads in the characteristic upside-down position, a pair of lesser flamingoes suck and sift algae from the calm soda shallows.

Flamingoes plane through the morning mist to join their flock on Lake Nakuru, while cormorants seem to act as sentinels in the trees.

6/ People from the Past

Most of the Rift, even the most brutally hostile parts of the Danakil
Depression, have for many thousands of years supported a complicated
pattern of tribes—Bantu peoples, Hamitics, Nilotics, Nilo-Hamitics.
Some of these are hunting peoples, others agriculturalists, many semi-
nomadic pastoralists, who rely on their cattle and goats. The Masai, who
range along the Rift in southern Kenya and Tanzania, are perhaps the
warrior pastoralists best known to the outside world. Today, even the
Masai are beginning to feel the pressures of so-called civilization. One
must look farther, to the remote and forbidding areas, to find tribes who
are virtually untouched by the 20th Century. In the parched landscape
that surrounds the shores of Lake Rudolf, several tribes, ethnically
widely different, eke out existences so primitive that they seem
survivals of the Stone Age. (The term "Stone Age" is not quite accurate
when applied to these people, since even the most remote tribes know
about metal, though they have not produced metal tools themselves.)
   The region around Lake Rudolf, the 195-mile long inland sea discovered by Count Samuel Teleki in 1887, is one of the most severe and
uncompromising, though often beautiful, wildernesses in the entire Rift
Valley. Very little grows along the lake's sandy, sterile western shore,
except where a rare fresh-water spring wells up and produces an oasis of
doum palms. Few large wild animals survive there. The eastern side is
quite different. A harsh rocky ledge is relieved by stretches of vivid

green reed bed, where zebra, oryx, lion, hartebeeste and waterbuck come to drink. But beyond the reeds stretches a country of pitiless dryness, gullied and eroded, with sparse scrub breaking up the grey volcanic earth and yellowish lake sediments. At the southern end of the finger-shaped lake, the water laps on the cruellest desert of all, a countryside of volcanic rocks bordered by sheets of knife-edge lava.

Yet in past ages, Rudolf was neither waterless nor barren. Its shores were teeming with wild animals including prehistoric elephants, three-toed ancestors of the horse, and game animals similar to those we know today. And by a strange irony it seems likely that here, where man now has to struggle for survival, some three million years ago hominids—early men-like creatures—took a vital evolutionary step along the path that led to *Homo sapiens*. Palaeontologists agree that, although Lake Rudolf and adjacent parts of the Rift may not necessarily be the only—or even the earliest—womb of mankind, this area has strong claims for primacy. Peking, Java and South Africa all have rival sites, backed up by fossil clues. But none of these geographical competitors has yet produced anything like the abundance of evidence that early, tool-using man evolved in what, today, seems an unlikely corner of the world.

The reason may simply be that 16 or more million years of unique geological history have created ideal conditions in the Rift Valley for preserving and revealing evidence that has been lost elsewhere—conditions ideal, first for fossilizing ancient bones, and, second for uncovering them by erosion or making them relatively easy for scientists to unearth. The past was encapsulated by the volcanoes that have played so active a part in the Rift's history, spewing out chemicals, such as calcium carbonate, that help turn bones into fossils. At the same time rifting created a chain of lakes whose levels rose and fell with the amount of rainfall. Some lakes were deepened by further faulting, and then obliterated by the lava flows that followed, while new ones were created by subsequent earth movements. Each new lake and each new lake-level laid down fresh layers of sediment, forming a complicated inter-layering of lava and sediment to capture and preserve bones until further upheavals brought them to light again, lifting up long concealed layers and exposing them to erosion.

It was here that the oldest hominid skull yet discovered was found by a young Kenyan anthropologist named Richard Leakey, son of celebrated parents, Louis and Mary Leakey, who had already uncovered much of early man's history in the Rift, notably in Tanzania. It was they who in the 1960s discovered the bones of a creature 1.8 million years old in Olduvai Gorge. Theirs was the oldest hominid find until 1972, when near Koobi Fora, at north-east Rudolf, Richard Leakey came upon a shattered cranium with genuinely humanoid characteristics simply lying on the surface in the grey-brown fossil beds. It appeared to have been washed out by recent rains. There is no problem about dating such finds—it is done by analysis of the traces of potassium argon gas found in them—especially if the bones have been fossilized in volcanic soil: Leakey's skull was 2.8 million years old.

Though the precise status of the skull has not been determined, and it is registered simply as "1470 man" by the National Museum of Kenya, scientists are in no doubt about the accuracy of the dating or that "1470", whose braincase was nearly as large as that of later ancestors of man, is indeed the earliest precursor of *Homo sapiens* yet found.

We can be reasonably sure how the owner of this skull looked and behaved. It is probable that he belonged to the same species as the hominids of Olduvai—*Australopithecus boisei*. These "men" stood under five feet tall, possessed low foreheads, bulging eyebrows and brains no bigger than that of a gorilla. Their molars were twice the width of our own, which suggests grinding teeth suited to a vegetarian diet. Most experts, including Leakey, believe that the Australopithecenes came to an evolutionary deadend and never made the all-essential leap to tool-making which led to the genus *Homo*, culminating in ourselves. Yet hundreds of stone axes and cutting tools have been found in the same area, so who *was* making stone tools on the shores of Lake Rudolf just over two and a half million years ago? There are many secrets locked up in the accumulated sediments of that wild and remote lake to which the key has yet to be found.

The scattered tribes that now live along Lake Rudolf's shores use techniques for living that are often not greatly different from those of the early hunters. The modern environment cannot support large numbers of land mammals, either animal or human. For peoples who are pastoral, with social organizations based on communal grazing land and water supplies, the problems of living in a region where rainfall is erratic and grazing land sparse are almost insuperable. Most of the tribes have been forced to become nomadic or semi-nomadic, with land held in common and individual ownership restricted to a man's herd of camels, cattle, sheep or goats. Surprisingly, only one tribe makes ends meet by fishing in the well-stocked waters of Lake Rudolf.

The lake is kept reasonably fresh by the river Omo, which flows in from the north through one of the strangest-looking deltas I have ever seen. It varies in extent according to the rainfall hundreds of miles away to the north on the Ethiopian high plateau, but its most unusual feature is the continuance of the river Omo three or four miles out into the lake, between high banks or levees. This canal-like formation, so regular that it appears almost man-made, is constructed by the river itself. As the Omo arrives, powerful and fresh, at its journey's end, the lighter, fresh water of the river floats on the heavier, sodary waters of the lake. As it thrusts into Rudolf, the river carries its sediments with it. After a short distance, the sediments at the edge of the Omo's current sink, building the first walls of the parallel levees. The river flows on between these banks, building an extension of the canal system for itself as it goes. Presumably there must be a limit, dictated by wave action, to this extending part of the delta, but there is little visible sign of destruction.

The three tribes that occupy the delta and the meander belts that stretch for 50 miles back to the Ethiopian and Sudan borders probably number not more than five or six thousand all told. These, the Desenech, the Bume and the Mursi, are the kind of ethnic mixture one would expect to find at a point sufficiently far north in the Rift to feel the strong tribal surge that sub-Saharan Africa has experienced from the Nile and Ethiopia. They are tall, dignified people, peaceful and stable enough within their own tribal frameworks, but fierce in defence of their territories and in their occasional raiding ventures on other tribes.

The Nilotic peoples—the Bume and the Mursi—probably come as near to the untouched primitive life as any people in Africa. Their bee-hive huts, very similar to those of the Danakil, 700 miles north, have a framework of bent saplings over which are laid hides or grass mats. The whole edifice is highly mobile, yet the village clusters of several hundred huts, interspersed with granaries built on stilts, are largely sedentary. The entire village is usually surrounded, like a walled city, by a single fence or even rings of barbed-wire-like, thorn defences, designed to keep stock in and enemies out.

Their farming is basic in the extreme, providing the village granaries with subsistence crops of sorghum, millet, beans and poor quality tobacco. Frequent bush fires suggest that they appreciate the value of regular burning to control old growth and encourage new, but, despite the sporadic flooding of the delta, they seem to know nothing of irrigation. They have, however, learned other uses for water: when flying low over the delta I have seen fishermen in dug-out canoes, a sophisticated form of water transport unknown throughout the length and breadth of

Turkana tribesmen wait patiently for fish on the shores of Lake Rudolf. When one of them spots a fish, he plunges his upside-down basket into

the water, trapping his victim against the lake bottom. He then puts his arm through the meshes and threads its gills with a reed.

the lake. The probable explanation is that the river provides them with trees large enough to be hollowed out with fire and axe.

The eastern shore of the great lake belongs to desert nomads, peoples of mainly Galla descent, Galla being the principal ethnic group of central and southern Ethiopia. It would take a whole faculty of professors of ethnology to sort out the precise tribal ancestries of the Rendille, the Kerre, the Banna, the Bachada, the Amarr, the Arbore and the Borana—north-east Rudolf peoples all. The most striking of these tribes are the Rendille, tall and proud people who wander the areas in which Richard Leakey made his great anthropological finds. They are camel people—it is said that, when a Rendille dies, his brother mourns him with one eye and counts his camels with the other—and are of warrior stock, given to tribal raiding.

But eastern Rudolf holds a greater menace than the Rendille: brigands, or the Shifta as they are known. The Shifta move in bands, like renegade Red Indians of the Old West, ready to kill and rob anyone whom they can outnumber or surprise. In 1965, a band of Shifta moved in on a small outpost called Loiengalani, at the south-east end of the lake, where some Europeans lived, and murdered three people, including the tourist lodge manager and a priest.

The two tribes I know best, however, are the Turkana, who live on the western shore, and the El Molo, sometimes called The Impoverished Ones, who are down at the southern tip. The Turkana are a jet-black people, with a majestic air that is utterly in contrast with the plight in which they now find themselves. Nomadic grazers of cattle, camels and goats, they have been increasingly hemmed in by the growing pressure on the land. In pre-colonial days, when they needed more space for their herds, they simply went out and seized it. They were cattle-rich—able to dole out as many as 40 head, plus other valuable goods, as a bride-price. But for the past century, because of rigidly defined tribal boundaries set up by the colonial government, they have been forbidden to expand their territory. At the same time, medicine has raised the population and veterinary services have tended to increase the survival rate of tribal cattle. Nomadic pastoralists seldom kill or sell their stock. To them, cows and goats are visible evidence of wealth and status. So there are more people and more stock and less food and grazing available. Not only that, but the landscape suffers from over-grazing; grass and scrub disappears, hooves cut up the topsoil, and erosion sets in. Thus, paradoxically, modern aids undermine the area's remaining resources.

Although there are now some 169,000 Turkana, about 13 times the number of Rendille, they have only a little more than twice the territory, and about one-third the number of camels and cattle. The situation is grave, and made even more so by the Turkana's insistence on the freedom of individual decision. The number of water holes, for instance, is extremely small. Yet the Turkana refuse to work co-operatively. There is no collective effort either to regulate or increase water stores.

Since 1962, the Kenya government has made great efforts to convince at least those Turkana who live closest to the lake to make the transition from their traditional pastoral life to that of fishermen. But to people who relish the taste of millet, blood and milk, fish is hardly a palatable substitute. There is an even more serious psychological problem: a man with no cattle is a man with no status. The Kenya Fisheries Department's programme has therefore moved along only haltingly. Fisheries' officers began by trying to teach the Turkana in the area of Ferguson's Gulf, halfway up Rudolf's western shore, to use boats and outboard motors. But water life is so alien that of 500 trained on the boats, only 200 stuck to fishing on a commercial basis. The rest returned to pastoral life within three years, and when an officer visited them to see how the experiment was progressing he found that many boats had been turned upside down and raised on stilts as dwelling places. Even the few who have continued to fish on a commercial rather than a mere subsistence basis regard the lake with awe and venture off-shore timidly. When the water is calm, handline or spear fishermen will kneel on rafts made of two palm logs bound together and, paddling with their hands, go out as far as several hundred yards. But no more. Their caution is justified. Rudolf is a lake of sudden gusting winds that come tearing out of the desert country to the north east, whipping up waves that can knock the life out of a small dinghy, let alone a dugout canoe or a palm-log raft.

So most Turkana prefer, if fish they must, to use another method taught them by the Fisheries people—gill-netting. They stand naked, lithe and black as obsidian, heaving nets and stone-weighted handlines into the breakers. Their feet do not appear to feel the heat stored in the yellow sand. Their primitive handlines are armed with forged steel hooks supplied by the Fisheries Department. And with these they bring in some truly giant Nile perch. I once watched a Turkana land one that comfortably topped the 100 pound mark, but that was no record. These fish, delicious to Western taste if not to the Turkana palate, often weigh as much as 200 pounds.

One form of Turkana fishery owes nothing to superimposed modern technology. I have stood at dusk on the shelving sandy shores and watched a reddish-yellow, will o' the wisp light dance along the reeded edge of a lagoon. Its glow catches the features of a Turkana as he stoops quickly towards the water. He bends and pauses and the light dips with his movements. Then he stands fully upright again. The light flickers a few paces closer along the shore, and the actions are repeated. I see now that the light comes from a smouldering bunch of dried reeds, a primitive torch used to attract fish. The Turkana's other hand holds a hemispherical, open-work basket made of bound saplings. In the hope that the light has lured to the surface fish who lurk among the reeds, he dips the basket at random, pausing each time to feel inside. At the seventh dip, his groping hand withdraws a small wriggling tilapia. Here is a method of fishing linking modern man to his Stone-Age ancestors.

Compared to the Turkana, the El Molo, living on the barren, pumice-strewn ridges at the southern end of the lake, are in a pitiable state. Beyond the great barrier of grey volcanic slag that hems them in, the ground drops away to a desolate frontier where no man lives, the Suguta Valley. Unlike the Turkana, the El Molo have always been fishers. The literal translation of their name is The People Who Live by Catching Fish. The tiniest and most depressed of all Rudolf's communities—numbering only about 270—they live in ragged round little huts made of grass and bits of driftwood that are so low that even their diminutive inhabitants must stoop to enter them.

Dr. John Hillaby, the English naturalist, visited them in the early 1960s, and felt as if he had been carried back into pre-history. "Rotting fish remains littered the ground; naked babies snatched at the flies; a few sticks upheld tattered nets. The impression was Neolithic."

Time has certainly wrought little change in their lives since Count Teleki first discovered them where they still are today, in the area of Loiengalani. At that time they lived exclusively on a little island just offshore, called Lorian, on which they had taken refuge from marauding tribes, especially the Turkana. Some of them still live on the island, ferrying their goats across to the mainland on rafts and feeding their few scrawny cattle on weeds dredged up from the shallows of the lake with their hands. But most have now returned to the mainland.

The El Molo pole about in the shallow edges of the lake on palm-log rafts, either spearing or netting fish. But unlike the Turkana, they are superb fishers. As harpooners of perch they are magnificent. There is something heron-like about the poise of an El Molo as he stands motionless with the quivering spear of hardened thorn root, detachable barbed tip attached to fibre line glinting as the sun strikes the metal. That metal tip is about the only concession that the El Molo, who not so long ago fashioned their harpoons from bone, make to the 20th Century.

South of the El Molo, and Loiengalani, where the ground drops away past razor-back bare hills into a nightmarish landscape of utter desolation, life seems almost to stop. There are no tracks across the southern end of the lake except ghostly-seeming trails picked out between lava boulders and knife-edged ridges by Turkana herdsmen. The winds that howl down the eastern shore of Rudolf mount in tempo throughout the early afternoon, increasing in violence into the night and finally exhausting themselves just before dawn.

It is in the no less hostile Suguta Valley, the "salt steppe" just to the south of this volcanic barrier, that Richard Leakey, flying his own light aircraft, has pinpointed strata that he hopes will yield some of the most dramatic traces of early man yet found.

At present there exists a break of ten million years in the hominid fossil record. There are no relics from this entire period except for a single crown of a nine-million-year-old molar found in the Tugen Hills near Lake Baringo. But layers of sediment and lava which Leakey glimpsed from his aircraft suggest that they may hide fossils that will bridge the gap. If such fossils are found, they will confirm Lake Rudolf's greatest irony. A place once lush enough to be the cradle for mankind has now been reduced by climate, geological change and animal grazing to a wilderness where man has to struggle to survive at all.

Into the Dark Continent in 1887

Count Samuel Teleki von Szek, a Hungarian sportsman, geographer and wildlife enthusiast, set out from Pangani on the east coast of Africa (map right) to work his way into the interior in January 1887. By that time, many of the dark continent's mysteries had already been plumbed. Lakes Victoria Nyanza and Tanganyika had been pinpointed and Lake Victoria identified as the source of the Nile.

But challenges remained. Teleki's companion and the chronicler of the expedition, Lt. Ludwig von Höhnel —from whose journal the engravings on these pages were taken and the text adapted—wrote, "our idea was to penetrate the then quite unknown districts on the north of Baringo, as yet unvisited even by native caravans, and in which some geographers said there was one lake, whilst others thought there were two big sheets of water".

For 22 months, the explorers penetrated jungles, swamps and lava-strewn volcanic plains in style. They travelled with a massive caravan that contrasted sharply with the improvised small-scale expeditions mounted by most European explorers. The party, financed by the Count himself, included some 450 porters, six guides and assorted translators, and was weighed down with 470 loads of trade goods for bartering with the Africans.

Although they made valuable observations on geology, geography and ethnology, they also spent considerable time satisfying their "hunting zeal". With the wanton passion that characterized explorers of their era, they shot everything from small fowl and antelope to hippopotami and elephants. Early in the trek they encountered their first leopard (opposite) which, in von Höhnel's bland words, "brought forcibly before my mind the fact that I was in Africa".

Though harassed by unfriendly natives, by extremes of temperature and by shortages of food and water, they ascertained that there were indeed two lakes. These Teleki named after Crown Prince Rudolf, heir to the Austro-Hungarian Empire, "who took the greatest interest in the expedition", and after Rudolf's wife, Stefanie. The expedition ended in Mombasa in October 1888.

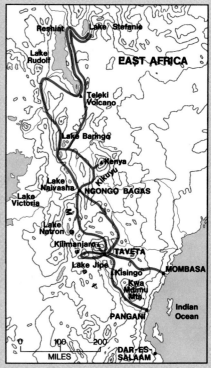

THE JOURNEY (OUT, RED; RETURN, GREEN)

FIRST ENCOUNTER WITH A LEOPARD

With Teleki to Rudolf

COUNT SAMUEL TELEKI VON SZEK

The first stages of our march quickly taught us how hot and thirsty one can become in East Africa. Worst of all was the terrain known to the natives as *nyika*–an uninhabited, barren, waterless, bushy steppe. The glare from the red laterite soil was terrible, and the dust was fearfully deep. The footprints of wild beasts proved that there was plenty of big game, but we shot little until we approached Mount Kilimanjaro. One morning, after almost three months, we set out in high spirits, for we expected to have our first glimpse of the snow-clad peaks of the mountain. The view was at first shut out by the heights jutting across the valley between the Kisingo and Kwa Mdimu mountains. But when these were left behind there was nothing to impede our vision. The whole valley was now spread out before us; on the west rose rugged mountains, gradually increasing in height. In the wide plain stretching to the east, we could see Lake Jipe, which looked like a narrow streak of light.

On this day Count Teleki had started earlier than the caravan, so as to do some hunting. He almost had more than he bargained for. Besides a successful double shot at two impala, he barely missed stumbling over a leopard. He had seen one in the high grass, but it disappeared too quickly for him to fire. Almost immediately he heard a growling nearby, and saw some animal approaching through the long grass. Thinking it was a wild boar, or something of that kind, he changed his rifle for a shotgun and fired. There was a rolling over and over in the grass, and then he saw the paws of a great leopard. He seized the rifle again; but the danger was past.

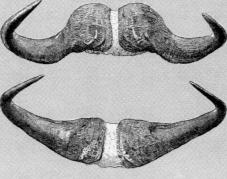

HORNS OF SLAUGHTERED BUFFALO

Some of his pellets had fortunately found a vital mark, and the animal lay dead.

The immediate neighbourhood of Lake Jipe, where this incident took place, is haunted by lions and leopards, giraffes, hyenas, ostriches and other wild creatures, which come down to the water to drink, so that it is a very paradise for the hunter. The lake itself abounds in crocodiles and hippopotami, as well as catfish and perch.

After almost three long months, only a few hours' march now separated us from the first goal of our journey, the forest-girt village of Taveta. Often the very sound of the name had acted like a magic spell upon our men, filling them, weary and worn as they were, with fresh hope, fresh energy. It was no wonder that now we were so near it we were all intoxicated with delightful anticipation! How much we might hope for in the beautiful quiet forest, into the depths of which we tried in vain to peer from the hill near the lake! What peace, what rest in the shade of this African paradise, beside murmuring streams, after our long tramp across arid steppes!

A Well-Guarded Entrance

As we neared the village the vegetation became greener and more luxuriant, the trees grew higher and closer together, the undergrowth denser and the parasites more numerous. At last we were utterly immersed in the dark, humid shades of the forest. The trees rose many feet above our heads, casting their long dark shadows across the path. Many a trunk lay right across the track, which wound in and out and backwards and forwards. We had to stoop and twist, to creep and crawl in single file, in order to avoid the many impediments in the way. Suddenly there was a shout of joy at the sound of distant firing—the signal that the head of the caravan had

A GERENUK

reached the entrance to Taveta, a door made of tree-trunks, closing the pathway to the settlement.

And now, like rolling thunder, the sounds of the firing of guns echoed on every side, startling hundreds of birds and terrifying the apes, which had been peering at us at close quarters. When the village door had been opened and we had made our way on all-fours through the narrow entrance, we could see better. The path led between tall hedges of banana-palms and across

MARABOU STORKS AND VULTURES COMPETING FOR A RHINOCEROS CARCASE

numerous little rivulets. Idle natives gazed at us in friendly fashion, whilst the women at work in the little wood-encircled fields paused to shout their greetings to us as if we were old friends: "*Yambo, Yambo, sana! Sabalcheir! Uhali ghani? Habari ghani?*" and so on, which meant, "Good day! God bless you! How are you? What's the news?"

As we intended to stop in Taveta for a long time, our first care was to get our camp in order. Some of the men cut away the weeds, while others dragged the tree-trunks and palm-leaf ribs with which to build the huts. In a few days we were the owners of a complete village, fitted out with stables for the donkeys and goats, a workshop and a kitchen.

The Local Inhabitants

We soon got to know the people of Taveta well. Every shady corner of our clearing was usually crowded with a chattering mob offering their wares for sale: fish, bananas, tobacco, honey, potatoes, sugar cane and now and then a hen. The first impression the Tavetans make is that they are extremely primitive, but nearer acquaintance proves that, like most of the tribes living near the well-organized Masai, they more or less closely resemble those handsome, semi-nomadic pastoralists.

This similarity is not surprising, for some 40 years ago the Tavetans were joined by a considerable number of Wakwafi, a branch of the great Masai family which had been decimated by civil war and dispersed. Deprived of their cattle, they had been forced to give up their accustomed pastoral life and were now scattered all round Masailand as tillers of the soil.

In Taveta, only the young copy the Masai style of costume in servile imitation. The young men, as a rule,

MAN OF TAVETA

wear only one garment—like the Masai. It is a short mantle of hairy goatskin of brownish red cotton stuff, which covers the left side of the body, and is fastened on the right shoulder. Now and then, they add a kind of leather apron to sit on that hangs down the back. Their hair is generally twisted into a number of thin, spiral locks that fall low on the forehead, sometimes down to the eyes. At the back it is lengthened with a plait of bark fibre which resembles a pigtail. The lobes of the ears are artificially widened, and decked with ornaments made of iron or brass wire, beads or iron chains. A few ornaments—bracelets around the wrists and ankles, mostly made of twisted wire or strips of leather sewn with beads—complete the costume. On the right side they wear a short, straight sword with a broad blade and on the other side swings a finely decorated wooden club.

The girls wear a petticoat of tanned and dressed goatskin, which sometimes hangs down below the thighs. The upper portion is often quite prettily trimmed with beads. They are particularly fond of neck ornaments, and sometimes wear necklaces made of more than 100 strings of beads twisted together; and the usual bracelets and anklets of brass and iron. In the widened lobes of their ears they insert a piece of fresh banana-leaf rolled up like a quill, or a round bit of wood. Both young women and men smear the nude portions of their bodies with a preparation of red earth and fat. In our eyes this presents a most terrible appearance; but to their fellows, a thick layer of grease gives them a delicate finish.

The older women wear, in addition to the petticoat, a second garment that partly covers the upper portion of the body; and some few ancient dames have lately adopted the cotton drapery, wrapped tightly about the bust in the style of the women of Zanzibar. One much-admired ear ornament worn by married men and women consists of thick brass wire wound in spirals till it forms a circle about four inches in diameter. Since these coils are too heavy for the lobe of the ear, they are partly supported by a band that rests upon the neck.

Circumcision is universally practised. Boys generally retire to the forest afterwards for a time, whilst girls, on whom a somewhat similar operation is inflicted, remain secluded for a month in their huts. If a stranger approaches, they hide their faces. The mothers of the girls smear their faces with streaks of red and white.

TAVETAN MARRIED WOMAN

From Taveta we made several excursions to visit the chiefs of two nearby tribes, the Chagga and the Meru, and to Mount Kilimanjaro, which Count Teleki climbed to over 15,000 feet. Then it was time for us to move on from Masailand.

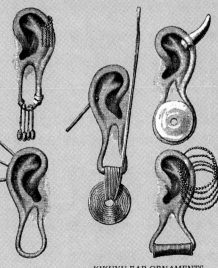

KIKUYU EAR ORNAMENTS

On August 27 we reached Ngongo Bagas, the spring of Bagas, an important camping place on the borders of Masailand and Kikuyuland. We had come to a vital stage in our journey. We stood upon the threshold of Kikuyuland, on the eve of a time full of trial and adventure.

Into Kikuyuland

Before our arrival, little was really known about the land or the people and countless tales were afloat of their fierceness and hostility. A caravan from Mombasa, it was said, had tried a few years ago to enter Kikuyuland from the east, and had been destroyed. Since then no traders had dared venture within range of the Kikuyu's poisoned arrows.

Fortunately an old Masai woman, named Nakairo, who was held in high esteem by the Kikuyu, happened to be in the camp, and she offered to be our intermediary. It is noteworthy that women on both sides are always perfectly safe in spite of the constant feud between the Masai and Kikuyu men. Knowing this we appointed the old lady to be our diplomatic agent. Although frightened by the white faces at first, the Kikuyu soon began to bring food and sell us their produce.

This people's lively, restless temperament is an indication of their relationship to the great Bantu stock. But physically they resemble the

Masai. Though they are seldom above medium height, they are well built, muscular and strong.

We only traversed the southern portion of the land inhabited by the Kikuyu, and as far as we can tell it stretches to the eastern base of Kenya and north to the equator.

To Mount Kenya

Our camp was not particularly beautiful scenery. About 100 paces off in a shallow ravine was a swamp overgrown with waterlilies and rushes, to which snipe and cranes came down now and then, whilst the croaking of frogs was continuous. Otherwise the district seemed deserted alike by men and animals.

We pitched our tents facing Mount Kenya, so that we might look at it

ORANGE-FLOWERED SENECIO JOHNSTONII

whenever the cloud canopy that generally shrouded it from view was lifted. Count Teleki was pressing on with his preparations for the ascent of the mountain and started on the morning of October 17 with five guides and 40 porters, leaving the rest of us behind in camp.

After his departure, it rained heavily. Woods and fields, which had been so dry and dreary-looking, were bursting with fresh life. It must, however, have been different in the lofty regions where Count Teleki now was. The mountain was continuously shrouded in gloomy clouds and heavy snow extended down the slopes. I was very anxious for the Count's return, but I need not have worried. His trip was perfectly successful. He ascended Mount Kenya to a height of 15,355 feet—all but the last two or three thousand feet— and ascertained the nature of its crater and slopes.

In his climb, he met many zebras,

elands and water-bucks, some longtailed apes and a leopard. "From nearly every cleft of the mountain," the Count reported, "flowed a little brook on the swampy banks of which grew various plants, some resembling the *Senecio johnstonii*, which bear large orange flowers." At 13,100 feet the Count saw the last animals of any size: a humming-bird, a pretty thrush-like bird and a hairy, tailless marmot.

After several months of journeying, from October 1887 to March 1888, we approached Lake Rudolf. There was a mighty mountain mass looming up before us. We hurried to the top of the ridge, the scene gradually developing until a new world spread out before us.

CRANES NEAR MOUNT KENYA

RARE OLEANDER-LIKE TREES

For a long time we gazed in speechless delight, spell-bound by the beauty of the scene. Our men, equally silent, stared into the distance, then broke into shouts of astonishment at the sight of the glittering expanse of the great lake which seemed to melt on the horizon into the deep blue of the sky.

The next day, after working our way through plains covered with black streams of lava, and dotted with craters from one of which clouds of smoke rose, we finally stood upon the beach of the lake. The beautiful water stretched away before us, clear as crystal. The men rushed down shouting, to plunge into the lake; but soon returned in bitter disappointment: the water was brackish! What a betrayal!

After several days, always in fear of hunger and thirst, we marched through a district where large herds of elephants lived. Several fell victim to our guns. Three we had wounded sought refuge in the lake, but by morning only one remained. So the Count sent three men out in our canvas boat. They were either to shoot the animal, or to drive him ashore. The boat circled the quarry, but the elephant did not budge an inch, no matter how many bullets struck his body. Suddenly, he charged furiously, and the men jumped

A WOUNDED ELEPHANT DESTROYING THE EXPEDITION'S BOAT

overboard. In the twinkling of an eye he was upon the fragile craft, which he seized with his trunk. He shook it, crushed it, tossed it about, and then contemptuously flung it aside. Finally, he marched with slow and stately steps through the water and disappeared behind a peninsula in the shoreline.

Making Friends with the Reshiat

After a month on Rudolf, we were full of delight at beginning our last march by the lake. We were off early, our men crying "Hurrah!" and "*Haya ugali!*" as they shouldered their loads. We would have shouted ourselves if previous experience had not taught us caution. But in spite of the assurances we had received of the friendliness of the Reshiat, the local tribe whom we were about to meet, we preferred not to make ourselves too much in evidence.

After an hour's walk we emerged from the wood that stretched westward, and came upon a stretch of ground strewn with human skulls and bones. This seemed ominously warlike. But a little later, we found ourselves amongst numerous herds of oxen and donkeys. The animals were grazing unguarded—a sure sign that the natives were peaceful.

This was perhaps the most interesting day of our whole journey, for we were now face to face with a perfectly unknown people. And the way in which these natives, who had hitherto lived quietly far away from the rest of the world, received us was so simple that we could not get over

our astonishment. First came a party of ten or twelve warriors, and behind them a group of some 60 or 80 men, who advanced fearlessly. They paused every now and then, but evidently not from nervousness, for they allowed the women laden with food to approach.

The chief of the village, a tall, slim man of about 50, recommended a camp site where we should be little bothered by mosquitoes and should have a pool of rainwater for drinking.

They sold us warm milk, beef, corn and tobacco, and our men got *ugali*, a stiff porridge, twice every day. Many supplemented this with fish and mussels, of which there were quantities in the lake, and with soft, sticky red berries. We encountered several kinds of fish, including one extraordinary species that resembled a snake, but with a coat of stiff, armour-like scales.

Our men now being fairly restored to health, we were once again seized with a longing for new discoveries and fresh experiences.

To Lake Stefanie and Back

After about a week's march eastwards from the northern tip of Lake Rudolf, and led by two guides who had only a vague notion of where the next sheet of water might be, we discovered a lake which we christened Lake Stefanie. It was shallow, barren and too brackish to drink, and surrounded by volcanic debris. We met no natives, and being short of supplies, left almost at once.

On the morning of April 25, we

pushed on along a path running parallel with the lake in a westerly direction. On this march the Count came upon a group of crocodiles, which rushed headlong for the water; not, however, before one of them had been shot dead.

As we marched further, we made the disagreeable discovery that it had not rained during the last few days. We obtained a little water by digging the next day, but no more after that. So we were compelled to do the whole of the march from Lake Stefanie to the village of Reshiat in four days. The last stage was no less than 25 miles, and we achieved it between daybreak and sunset, with only one short interval for rest.

The Homeward Journey

On the evening of May 27 we returned to our camping-place of March 12. Although we had only marched for 14 days since leaving Reshiat, and eight rhinoceroses with one zebra had been added to our stores of food, not one of our men had a scrap of their rations left.

We pressed on along the shore, reaching our old camping-place at the southern end of Lake Rudolf on the evening of May 31. We had done the 235 miles in 16 days of 90 marching hours, whereas the same distance had taken 28 days going up. The fears of food shortage with which we had started southwards had not, most fortunately, been realized. So far fate had been kind to us, and, full of fresh hope, we set off for far-distant Mombasa.

THE CAMP AT THE SOUTHERN END OF LAKE RUDOLF

7/ The Elephants of Manyara

*Elephants breed in that part of Affricke which lyeth beyond
the deserts. . . . Wonderful is the wit and subtiltie that these
dumb creatures have and how they shift for themselves.*

PLINY/ *HISTORIA NATURALIS*

My journey down the Rift began in the Danakil desert, as stark and
inhospitable a landscape as anywhere on earth; it was appropriate that
it ended with a complete contrast: a visit to the lush forests and
savannah of Manyara, 80 miles south of Lake Natron.

The area below the escarpment at Manyara is possibly the most
luxuriant place in the whole East African Rift. Its soil grows anything
from elephants to bananas, from rhinos to pawpaws. Much of the area is
a National Park, one of the few actually in the Rift. But it nevertheless
represents Africa at its wildest, as anyone who has lived under canvas
and worked down there will testify. I once came back to my tent after a
few minutes' absence to find that four lions had sacked the place and
dragged all the bedding out into the open. The sheets were still wet with
saliva and jagged with tooth marks. The park itself—30 miles along
Lake Manyara's western shoreline—and the surrounding area is also the
one place in the entire valley where large numbers of elephant roam. It
has an average of 12 elephants per square mile, the greatest concentration of elephants in Africa.

The park, bordered on the east by the alkaline waters of Lake
Manyara, runs on its western side up into the Manyara escarpment.
Other escarpments may be higher but few have the magic of Manyara.
The tree-covered, often nearly vertical slope plunges down, sometimes to
within a few hundred yards of, and seldom more than four miles from,

the lake shore. The scarp is fissured by a series of twisting gorges. Between these, forested buttresses project into the savannah beneath. I have flown down some of those gorges with Alan Root who has often been forced to bank the plane at an angle of 45 degrees to negotiate the next turn. In places, these ravines are barely half again as wide as the wing-span of the aircraft. It makes for interesting flying.

On one occasion we took a gorge unknown to Alan. Several flat-topped huts hanging on the face of the chasm proclaimed that Sonjo tribesmen lived there. The Sonjo, an agricultural, Bantu-speaking people, comparatively light in colour, once lived in terror of the dark-skinned, warlike Masai and so built their homes underground to hide them from raiding warriors. The need has receded but a remnant of the tradition remains. The huts from whose roofs we raised the red dust were, I noticed with what eyes the hair-raising flight left me for anthropological observation, half buried in the soil. These Sonjos had evidently never seen an aircraft before. When we bellowed through their pass, they took to the cellars, as did their chickens and, I believe, one goat, almost as if the Masai had taken to the warpath once again.

Observations from the ground are somewhat less nerve-racking but equally informative. Driving from the escarpment on the rough road down to the forests and plains below, it is easy to see why so many elephants and other animals live there. The road runs into an area of well-watered forest. Many streams, clearer than the purest trout streams, run down from the escarpment just here and so maintain a constant and fairly high level of ground water. Springs well up throughout the forest. Water is generally an element to beware of in Africa. Close to habitation and, especially when slow-running, it is almost certain to contain human effluent, one of the carriers of bilharzia parasites which eventually attack liver and intestines. But no menace hides in this pure water. It is perfectly safe to bathe in it, drink it, and eat the succulent water cress that grows alongside it, planted years ago by some European with memories of English high teas and summer salads.

The forest itself evokes memories of Tarzan. It is green and cool. Among its trees, the magnificent figs and African mahoganies are taller than English oaks and beeches and far more luxuriant. The savannah just beyond the forest grows many kinds of acacia, notably *Acacia tortilis*, and also *Acacia clavigeria*, the stinkbark, whose aromatic scent is to elephants what aniseed is said to be to dogs. Near the lower part of the scarp, one tree dominates by size and stature, *Adansonia digitata*, the baobab. Several African tribes believe that the baobab is the home of night spirits. One legend declares that God was angry with the tree and planted it upside down. Its trunk is bulbous, and its branches do have an upside-down look. Baobabs are soft-tissued, fleshy, and frequently full of holes excavated by birds and small mammals. They support and offer temporary home to everything from eagles to arboreal snakes. At night they are visited by bats that help to pollinate their ghostly white blossoms. Big-eyed bush babies creep around their branches in the dusk. It is small wonder that the baobabs have found their way into legend as the homes of ever-active night spirits.

The luxuriant forest supports a rich variety of animals. Lions lie idle along branches, cooling in the breeze and escaping the attentions of biting flies. Baboons shake themselves from the trees like ripe fruits. Blue Syke's monkeys swing and leap, using the creepers as trapezes. A heart-stopping crash and tearing, close at hand, announces elephant; the dense ground cover makes it impossible to see how many, even at 30 yards. Nearby in a small open space, a black rhino cow, wallowing in a spring, snorts and throws its head from side to side, searching with its nose for what may be an enemy and deciding in the primeval darkness of its mind whether it should bother to charge or not. Black rhinos, as unstoppable once in motion as a runaway locomotive, are totally unpredictable. Fortunately they are also short-sighted. Often they cannot focus clearly on the target and thus lose at least 50 per cent of the opportunities for throwing their one and a half tons about.

Where the springs cease, the dense forest ceases also. More open savannah begins. It, too, is amazingly green, and its scattered stands of trees are usually in leaf before the rains start. The run-off from the escarpment makes its influence felt here, even if not in quite such an obvious way. The soil, brought down over thousands of years from the highlands, is ready to grow practically anything.

Among the trees of the savannah, *Acacia tortilis* is the one Manyara elephants like to eat before all others. *Tortilis* is a beautiful flat-topped tree. Just before the rainy season it blossoms with white flowers that baboons appreciate, and in the dry season it is hung with yellow seed pods to which elephants are addicted. At that season the Manyara elephants go on an *Acacia tortilis* binge, butting the tree trunks with their four-ton bulk until the acacia sheds its pods in golden rain. An elephant's trunk is a remarkably precise instrument. It can pick up an acacia pod with a delicacy matching that of a sunbird selecting a single blossom from which to sip nectar.

An alert group of impala browses through lush undergrowth around Lake Manyara. The impressive horns of the male are mainly for courtship show: these graceful antelope rely on keen noses and wide ears for early warning of cheetah or leopard. Once alarmed, they scatter in a jumping, jinking retreat.

Though the elephants do much to destroy their acacia habitat, they also perform a vital role in its regeneration. Their predilection for the tree's fruit—a single elephant may contain in its intestines at any one time more than 10,000 *Acacia tortilis* seeds—provides *tortilis* with easily its most effective method of propagation. Unlike other trees, such as the sycamore which relies on the wind to disperse its seeds or the oak which enlists the burying activities of squirrels, *Acacia tortilis* is regenerated through the guts and droppings of elephants. There are two schools of thought about how the cycle works, but both conclude that unless the seeds pass through the elephants' alimentary canals, they are unlikely to germinate. One theory places emphasis on the elephants' stomach. It compares the seed to a time-bomb whose firing mechanism is at "safe". If it simply falls from the tree to the ground, the seed is considered to be unarmed and does not explode into life. But, just as some time-bombs are detonated by the action of acid eating away a fine copper wire to release the firing pin, so *Acacia tortilis* is said to have its own detonation mechanism—the acid in the digestive juices which eats away the seed's outer casing. By the time it reaches the ground encased in a dropping, the seed is fully sensitized and ready to germinate. A more recent theory argues that the key factor is the movement of the animal. According to this, the seed is unlikely to germinate in the shadow of its parent tree. What counts is not the eating away by acid but the dispersal of the seed to places where there is adequate light.

I have seen the Manyara bush littered with the nine-inch bulbs of dried elephant droppings from which the small, pea-like leaves of *tortilis* shoots are already emerging. The process of regeneration at Manyara is continuous and lively, but by no means sufficient on its own to keep pace with increasing demands from the elephant population.

To me, elephants are certainly the most impressive wild animals left in the world. At Manyara, there are some individual animals I am never likely to forget, individuals I learned to know in the company of 27-year-old Dr. Iain Douglas-Hamilton and his wife, Oria, who had then already spent five years studying the behaviour and movements of every elephant among the 500 or so that live in Manyara.

The work was essential for the elephants' own preservation. Here was a dense pocket of the largest land animals in creation living free, or almost free. Hemmed in by the steep wall of the Rift to the west, with the lake shore to their east, they have only this narrow, albeit extremely fertile band of country to call their own. At times, particularly during

Many animals of the Rift are so elusive that often the only signs of their presence are the footprints left in the soft mud of waterholes. A massive paw mark (top left) testifies to the silent visit of a leopard by night. The tiny hoofprint (top right) was left by a dik-dik, an antelope the size of a fox, and the slightly larger though similar one (bottom left) by a stately gazelle. Four long fingers and distinct nail marks identify the firm imprint of a baboon (bottom right).

LEOPARD

DIK-DIK

GAZELLE

BABOON

the dry season, they must leave it to find food elsewhere, following age-old migration routes up the Rift wall into the forests on top. Man closes the borders to north and south with farmland, cutting the routes. In the north, beyond the rich ground water forest lies the village of Mto-wa-Mbu ("the river where the mosquitoes live"). Here the red soil grows bananas and could grow any crop the local citizens cared to plant. To the south there are farms again, farms originally wrested out of the bush by the strength and capital of Europeans, who were given a concession to cultivate this land on the frontier of elephant country. The elephants, naturally, are no respecters of such frontiers and the farmers shoot them in defence of their hard-won crops.

In this way Manyara's elephants mirror the universal problems facing all wild elephants left in the world. If they follow their traditional migration patterns in search of food, they will clash with man and in all probability get shot. If they are forced to stay where they are, they may eat themselves out of food. Such ecological disasters have already happened in other parts of Africa. Once the trees go, everything else, grass, soil, a way of life and of living for most large wild animals is likely to follow. Only the wrinkled face of erosion remains. It was Douglas-Hamilton's task to consider this unhappy juxtaposition of interests and, if possible, come up with a solution.

To study how elephants fit into their environment it is necessary to understand their social structure, migration patterns and details of fecundity and age. This had been attempted before, in other elephant crisis areas such as Murchison Falls Park, in Uganda, where 12,000 elephants confined inside 1,500 square miles have left hardly a tree intact; and in Tsavo, in Kenya, where exactly the same environmental tragedy is being enacted. In these studies, research into the elephants' social behaviour had been attempted by shooting and dissecting whole family herds. This drastic procedure was partly justified by the clear need to reduce the population and thus protect the depleted food sources, but mainly because it seemed the only way of arriving at some scientific conclusions. But at Manyara, the soil is so productive that if the elephants' requirements, in terms of population distribution, freedom of movement and birth rate, are understood in time, culling may never be necessary. It was essential, therefore, to find out how the elephants lived and moved and what could be done to preserve their living space as a sound ecological unit.

Douglas-Hamilton resolved that he would perform the whole study, no matter how long it took, without killing a single elephant. First, he and his wife had to devise a method of recognizing every cow elephant—cows are the basis of elephant society. They proceeded to build up a file of recognition photographs, close-ups that gave details of individual characteristics, even down to small notches and tears in the ears. Since the elephant fully extends its ears only when it is making a threatening demonstration, this usually meant persuading the beasts to make a charge at close quarters. Then Douglas-Hamilton had to condition the different family units to know and accept him so that he could move among them, sometimes on foot, for observation.

Next Douglas-Hamilton needed to know the distribution of age within elephant groups, a goal achieved by laboriously estimating the age of each elephant in the forest. There is a direct relationship between height at the shoulder and age. The only problem was how to gauge the shoulder height of a wild African elephant. Douglas-Hamilton built a photographic height-finder. Two mirrors at the ends of a long metal arm reflected their twin images through a prism to a 35mm camera. Each elephant photographed therefore appeared as a double image. From this double image he was able to calculate—in the same way as an artillery range-finder determines distance—shoulder height to within the very fine limits of an inch either way.

Gradually, the dossier on Manyara elephants accumulated until every cow was known, logged, photographed, and given a name, so that the habits and movements of it and its group could be followed throughout the year. The structure of elephant society is a matriarchal one. Possibly this is more in evidence here than anywhere else in Africa. Under stress conditions—when food is short, for instance—the family groups spread out and individual members scatter. At Manyara, despite the pressure of over 500 elephants on a comparatively small habitat, there is seldom real shortage and the family groups keep together, under the rule of the matriarchs. (Bull elephants, despite their fearsome reputation in fiction, are not masters of their fellows but noisy cowards that trumpet, scream and false-charge on principle but very seldom mean it.) The senior cows, however, are something different.

The most impressive matriarch at Manyara at the time of my visit in 1973 was Boadicea, as Douglas-Hamilton had named her. She was certainly the most imposing elephant I ever met. Boadicea was about 45 years old, of enormous height and beautifully proportioned. Her ivory, though not especially thick or heavy, was long and symmetrical. She was totally in command of her large group of 20 or so beasts, including several small calves. Lesser matriarchs like Diana, with a broken tip to one tusk, Virgo, a one-tusked elephant from birth, and the enormous Right Hook, relied on Boadicea for leadership and protection.

I accompanied Douglas-Hamilton as he studied Boadicea. She never once took her eyes off us, and when we approached close in our derelict, open-topped Land Rover, charged with a display of ferocity that frightened me very much. Boadicea commanded the full repertoire of vocal and visual intimidation. Her first demonstration, at a range of around 50 yards, was to shake clouds of dust off her ears. Then, as we got closer, she rushed towards us at great speed, trumpeting and growling, head down, trunk down, tusks lowered to hook the enemy if he did not turn away. "Elephants have spent a few million years perfecting their threat charges", Douglas-Hamilton commented; "they mean them to be impressive".

The daily routine of Boadicea's unit is typical of life in an elephant cow herd. While the matriarch takes over all responsibility for leadership, lesser ladies perform nursery chores. Females approaching sexual maturity, and those just past it, can frequently be seen waking up young elephant that have fallen asleep in the grass and failed to realize the group is moving on. Discipline is impressed on the young, especially young males, from an early age. A calf that tries to push in at the small holes, which elephants dig in dry stream-beds, to allow water to filter up through the sand, is liable to be slapped, pushed with a leg or rump and often sent sprawling to make it learn its place.

The cows communicate a good deal within the group with a language of deep rumbling growls made in the throat. They may also communicate with what is called a kinship group, usually composed of more distant blood relations, which are likely to be cruising the bush in their own loose formation half a mile or so away. A group's reaction to alarm signals from the matriarch in charge is enough to discourage the most redoubtable enemy. The cows form a phalanx—tusks flailing bushes, heads swaying, the air torn with screams and growls—or, when caught on open savannah, frequently make a defensive circle. Calves are tucked in, hidden by clouds of dust stirred up by the restless shuffling of a forest of adults' legs. I personally would be willing to face such a gathering in nothing less than a tank.

Bulls live a quite different life. At Manyara, adult males are frequently to be found along the lake shore, either singly or in small bachelor parties. The largest all-male group I have encountered is ten. Sometimes

An elephant applies the full force of its trunk and tusks to fell a small tree, and so reach the succulent foliage above. Elephants are constantly ripping off branches and bark in their quest for food and moisture, and they often destroy large numbers of trees in times of drought when there is little nutritious vegetation remaining on the ground.

a pair of bulls can be seen 150 yards or more out in the lake, pushing and shoving at each other in the manner of playful bathers, their tusks gleaming white in the water like the newly cleaned teeth they are. And, as they press along in water three or four feet deep, the bow wave they throw up is blue-green with the familiar diatoms that multiply so abundantly in an alkaline lake.

Play-fighting between bulls starts at an early age. It is a vital activity that establishes their place in elephant society, their precedence over other bulls when it comes to food, water and sex. The first play-fighting is little more than a nursery romp that takes place within the herd and is often broken up by the cows which, like mothers and grandmothers everywhere, know when enough is enough. I watched a Manyara cow stop a prolonged fight between two largish bulls, perhaps ten-year-olds, and a precocious youth half their size. This infant had nothing to do with the original scrap but, whenever the action seemed about to slow up, intervened with a butt or two at one of the principals to get them going again. In the end a large adult cow strolled across and pushed the three apart simply by walking straight through them. Whether the smallest calf was its offspring or not I don't know, though I suspect it was. Anyway, the cow reassured the calf by putting a maternal trunk in its mouth, that most touching of elephant gestures.

At puberty, around 13 years of age, the young bull's days with the female family group come to a close. The male becomes a nuisance and its biological function must soon be fulfilled elsewhere. It turns into a rover, free to wander and mate with any cow, from any group that will accept it. Acceptance depends on his achieving sufficient status. For the last few years of group life the maturing male is increasingly chivvied by the cows until even its bullheaded nature begins to take the hint. It is not wanted. The umbilical cord stretches, but for some time does not break. At first it hangs around within sight of the heaving backs of its former family unit as they roll across the bush like a flotilla of grey battleships, hull down on the horizon. Gradually, the distance lengthens. Play-fighting with other outcasts of similar age and weight continues. The male jousts with the young knights it meets on its travels and the challenges are offered and met with more serious intent as time passes. I have heard the clash of ivory upon ivory on occasions from a half a mile away, long before reaching the scene of the battle. It seems incredible that more damage is not inflicted in these contests. One often sees elephants with body sores made by tusk wounds. But eyes, surely the most vulnerable part in a frontal attack, seem never to be harmed.

Lake Manyara's 500 elephants are divided into small, closely-knit family groups, led by the strongest, most experienced cows, a system that provides a secure matriarchal framework for calves, sick herd members and adolescent bulls as they prepare in play-fighting for a future away from the herd.

MATRIARCH THREATENING TO CHARGE

CALF SEEKING SECURITY

PROTECTIVE GROUP AROUND SICK ELEPHANT

YOUNG BULLS SPARRING

Much of the detail of herd life can be learned by close observation on foot and in a skilfully handled Land Rover. Iain Douglas-Hamilton has built up his picture of the Manyara herds mainly by these methods. But a wider picture of elephant group movement over a period of, say, a year can be obtained only by telemetry—tracking the bleep-bleep signals emitted from a small transistorized radio transmitter attached to the animal concerned. Telemetry in wildlife study is now a well-established method and has been practised on everything from peccaries to rhinos. The co-operation of a large and dangerous animal, necessary for attaching the transmitter, can be obtained only by darting it—knocking it out with a hypodermic syringe-dart filled with anaesthetic and fired from a gun. Not more than 20 minutes later it must be injected with tranquillizer to bring it round. The tranquillizer counteracts the anaesthetic to prevent prolonged immobility, which could damage an elephant in a number of ways. The sheer weight of a collapsed elephant on its lungs and rib-cage is one hazard. Another is the effect of sunlight reaching the retina of the eye through a dilated pupil that can no longer react to bright light. In addition, the elephant can no longer flap its ears—an action that helps dissipate body heat—and it may suffer heat-stroke.

Douglas-Hamilton decided that the easiest way to keep tabs on the annual peregrinations of a cow herd was to fix a radio to a recently evicted young bull. Since the bull would move where the herd moved, without being part of the herd, it would be an exact indicator of their wanderings. To have darted one of the cows, Iain reasoned, would have been unnecessarily dangerous, if not impossible, since the attendant matriarchs would be unlikely to leave the distressed animal. Much more than the risk to himself, Iain was concerned about the disturbance caused to the herd by such a darting. The experiment was to demonstrate dramatically how true this assumption was and how closely knit were the family groups of Manyara elephants.

The first part of the experiment went according to plan and produced the results expected. By tracking radio-carrying bulls on foot and in his own aircraft, Douglas-Hamilton was able to show how the wanderings of several herds were related to the availability of food. But he had a limited number of transmitters and so had to dart each bull a second time when he wanted a radio back to transfer it to another animal. It was one of these second dartings that caused an incident illustrating the close social ties and loyalties evolved for the mutual protection of herd members, relationships extended even to an evicted bull.

The bull in question belonged to a herd supervised by a very large matriarch called Sarah, whose appearance was all the more intimidating because the last 18 inches of her tusks were crossed. But the selected male was apparently on its own and when Douglas-Hamilton found it wearing the desired radio, he darted it according to plan. The animal staggered off under the influence of the drug and Douglas-Hamilton prepared to wait the usual 20 minutes for the anaesthetic to take full effect. Only a few minutes had passed before there was trumpeting and crashing of bushes. Presumably the darted bull had made some alarm call, for Sarah and four senior females of her group had come to the drugged bull's rescue. Here was a first-hand demonstration of what might have happened had Iain chosen to dart a member of a cow herd. But if this turn of events was potentially dangerous to a human researcher, it was an immediate and far more serious threat to the bull. If Sarah and her companions continued to guard the bull—and there seemed no earthly reason why they should change their minds—there would be little chance of injecting the tranquillizer that must follow darting within a very short time if the animal is not to suffer serious damage. Iain had no spare darts so there could be no question of injecting the tranquillizer from a safe distance.

Sarah and her attendant cows, seriously distressed, tried to lift the partially unconscious bull to its feet. It weighed well over a ton and so their efforts were, not surprisingly, in vain. Douglas-Hamilton now made several attempts to approach on foot with a hyperdermic full of tranquillizer. Each time he only just escaped Sarah's charge. She would probably have smashed him to pulp had she not stopped short to return to the unconscious bull.

Finally, he got back into his Land Rover, drove it into the centre of the furious cows and just had time to inject half a dose of tranquillizer into the bull before Sarah charged, driving her tusks first through the radiator and then up and over the bonnet, demolishing the screen and steering wheel and narrowly missing Douglas-Hamilton. To avoid those crossed tusks he lunged back so hard that he broke the Land Rover's seat from its anchorage, a feat of some desperation, not to say strength. The vehicle, impelled by Sarah's tusks, shot backwards at around 20 m.p.h. and hit a tree. Mercifully, Sarah withdrew at this point, plainly under the impression that such an application of force had killed her enemy. Iain was still not satisfied and took advantage of her withdrawal to run in on foot and inject the rest of the antidote. The bull recovered and made off—very much alive, but with the precious radio still attached—a testimony to the elephants' corporate family sense.

The Manyara elephant research project, though special to the region's particular problems, has widespread application to the tragic situation in which elephants find themselves all over Africa. And it has led to two solutions, one of which has already been put into use.

After radio-tracking showed how dense the elephant concentrations are at the north end of the Park, where Mto-wa-mbu farmers grow bananas, a special elephant delicacy, Douglas-Hamilton set out to protect the banana *shambas* from the elephants—and the elephants from the *shamba* owners. He put up a single-strand electric fence, similar to those used for controlling cattle on farmland. At first the matriarchs tore the trial fence down. But they soon learned that the mild shock they received at the tip of their trunks was distasteful and a sensation to be avoided. Today, a stout, three-strand electric fence guards the banana frontier. Though a few smart elephants find that they can outflank the defences by walking a mile or two round the end of the wire, the effectiveness of this deterrent is enhanced by the fact that the elephants have to ford a stream between forest and bananas immediately before they reach the wire. The shock—though still a relatively mild and harmless one—is that much more convincing because the elephants are still wet from their crossing.

An electric fence works only where the frontier to be guarded is a relatively short one, as here in the north, for the wire has to be patrolled two or three times a day to check for breakages. At the southern end, the situation is quite different. Here again, radio-tracking has pointed the way to a long-term answer.

To the south lie the farms allocated to European farmers in the late 1950s. At that time, conservationists questioned the wisdom of anyone trying to farm with 500 wild elephants as next door neighbours. Nevertheless the farmers went ahead, cleared the virgin bush and planted coffee, pawpaws, maize and millet, which prospered in the fertile soil below the Rift wall. And the elephants, as expected, came to help harvest the crops and, as expected, got shot. More damaging to the elephant herds than a few casualties was the location of the farmland athwart their migration route to the wall of the Rift. Only a few trails are left open and as a result these five-ton animals climb tracks more suited to the agility of baboons in order to reach 90 square miles of rich forest, the Marang Forest Reserve, that lies over the crest of the Rift and supplies food when their home grounds are overgrazed during the dry season.

Dr. Douglas-Hamilton's work has made the importance of this migration route plain to all. Now there is some hope that Tanzania will be able to buy those farmlands back. If this happens, wild animals, will, for once, have won. Manyara will have become a viable ecological unit of plains and forest which can more than contain the highest concentration of elephants left in Africa.

One of the steepest of these remaining paths into the forest rises close to a place called Endabash, where a waterfall cascades hundreds of feet from rocks above. This track taxes human legs and stamina. Yet the huge animals climb it in order to enjoy the forest beyond the crest. It is a magic place to visit, but one to be approached with caution. The bush is thick and it is an excellent spot in which to surprise—or bad spot in which to be surprised by—elephant. The elephants of Endabash are of an unpredictable nature. So many of them have been shot, or at any rate shot at, they may take any human to be an enemy.

Manyara is a fitting place at which to end my journey down the Rift Valley wilderness. Though in a geological sense the Rift continues southward, its nature from here onwards is very different. Geologists can follow its progress, but it no longer retains the unity that makes the stretch from the Red Sea to Tanzania so fascinating.

It is as if the underlying grain of Africa has changed. Like an old and gnarled piece of timber, the cracks in the Rift do not always run true. And if two terms sum up the Great Rift Valley they are precisely those: old, old as the green hills of Africa and gnarled as only 20 million years of earth history can make it.

The Moment of Fear

The "balance of nature" is a phrase much used by nature lovers, but in fact nature is never in balance. Always some influence is at work depressing the scales on one side or the other: climatic change, geological upheaval, a new evolutionary advantage that allows one species to thrive at the expense of another. The Rift Valley has known many such changes in its 20-million-year history. Yet recently, in the latest blink of time's eyelid, one pressure above all has weighted the scales against wildlife there—the hand of man.

For thousands of years, African tribesmen lived more or less in harmony with the elephant and the buffalo, the lion and the antelope, taking only what they needed for survival and what they could get with spear or arrow. But in the late 19th Century, British and German explorers introduced the firearm and indulged in massive slaughter: for sport, for trophies, to make way for agriculture, or for gain. The European remorselessly hunted and largely shot out the Rift's great herds of game. Those animals that remain have learned to avoid mankind, and in doing so have discovered a reaction that they never knew before: fear.

The hand of man is of course responsible for the remarkable portraits on these pages; and although it is man's harmless camera rather than his weapon that is aimed at the prey, the subject of the portrait in each case has been caught at that moment of fear as it reacts to the alien presence with understandable caution, stealthiness or abrupt retreat.

Thus the gerenuk raises its long neck cautiously to browse among bushtops, its ears straining to locate the source of the camera's click. From an even loftier viewpoint, giraffes pause, immobile and suspicious at the photographer's intrusion. A herd of restless, ever-moving gnu panic and stampede, stirring clouds of dust from galloping hoofs.

The ponderous hippos have learned that in daytime they are safe only in the sun-silvered waters of the lake. The jackal slinks by the photographer to disappear hastily in the golden grass. Splashing waterbuck and leaping eland rely on speed to give man a wide berth. The lion caught in the lights of a passing vehicle, or even approached in daylight, will quickly retreat, knowing by bitter experience that man's arsenal of weapons—and therefore man—is the greatest danger to the wild inhabitants of the Great Rift Valley.

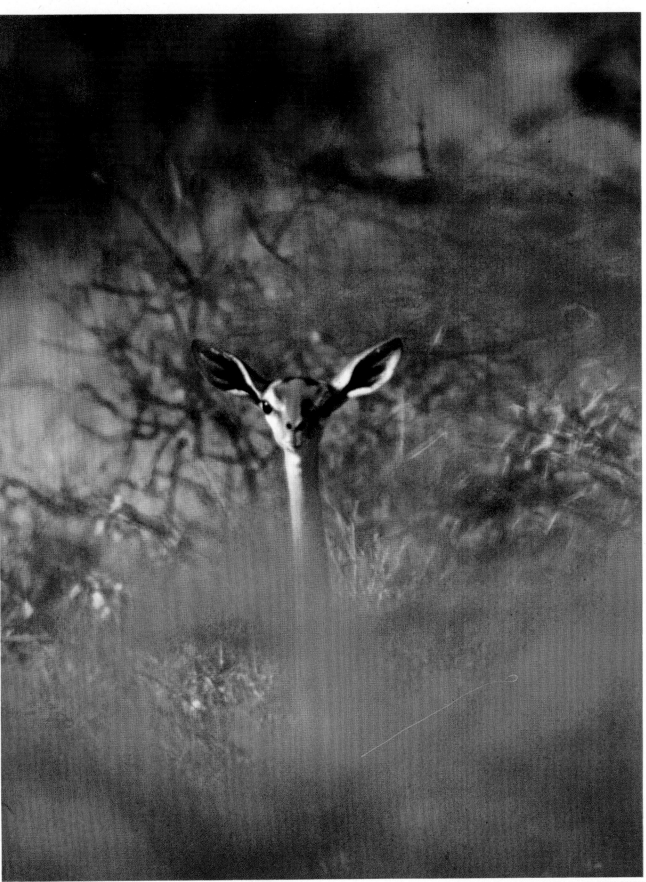

A NERVOUS GERENUK PEERING FROM THE BUSH

GIRAFFES IN STATELY SOLITUDE

FLEEING WILDEBEEST

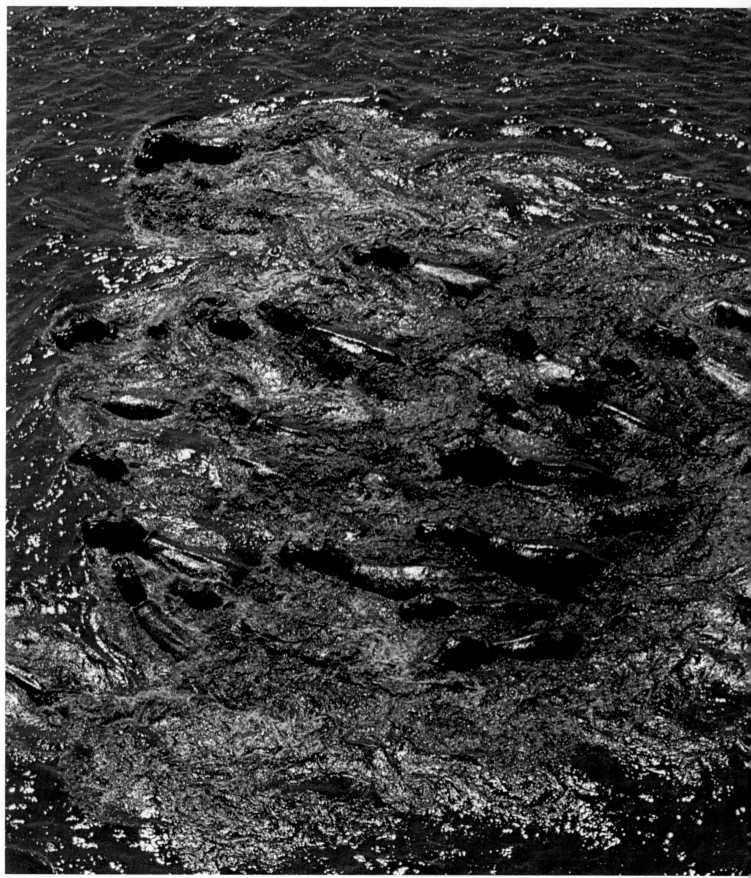

HIPPOS SWIMMING IN FORMATION

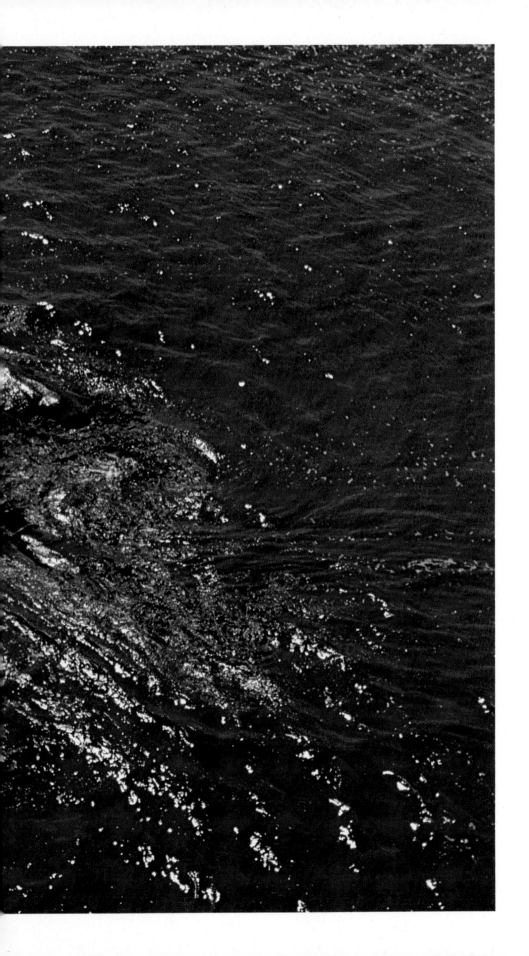

A JACKAL STALKING ITS PREY

A SPLASHING WATERBUCK

AN ELAND IN MID-LEAP

A HUNTING LIONESS SURPRISED BY A CAMERA FLASH

Bibliography

Alexander, T., "The Wandering Continents", *Nature/Science Annual*. Time-Life, 1970.

Astley-Maberley, C. T., *Animals of East Africa*. Howard Timmins, 1960.

Beadle, L. C., *Inland Waters of Tropical Africa. An Introduction to Tropical Limnology*. Longman, 1973.

Beckinsale, R. P., *Land, Air and Ocean*. Camelot Press, 1966.

Brown, L., *Africa: A Natural History*. Hamish Hamilton, 1965.

Brown, L., *The Mystery of the Flamingoes*. Country Life Books (The Hamlyn Publishing Group Ltd.), 1959.

Chapman, A., *On Safari*. Edward Arnold, 1908.

Cole, S., *The Prehistory of East Africa*. Weidenfeld and Nicolson, 1964.

Cox, R., *Kenyatta's Country*. Hutchinson, 1965.

Drury, G. H., *The Face of the Earth*. Penguin, 1959.

Edey, M. A., *The Missing Link*. Time-Life Books, 1972.

Fryer, G. and Iles, T. D., *The Cichlid Fishes of the Great Lakes of Africa*. Oliver and Boyd, 1972.

Fuertes, L. A. and Osgood, W. H., *Artist and Naturalist in Ethiopia*. Doubleday, 1936.

Green, T., *The Adventurers*. Michael Joseph, 1970.

Gregory, J. W., *The Great Rift Valley*. John Murray, 1896.

Gregory, J. W., *The Rift Valleys and Geology of East Africa*. Seeley, Service and Co., 1921.

Hemingway, E., *The Green Hills of Africa*. Penguin, 1972.

Hill, M. F., *Magadi*. The Kynoch Press, 1964.

Hillaby, J., *Journey to the Jade Sea*. Constable, 1964.

Höhnel, L. R. von, *The Discovery of Lakes Rudolf and Stefanie*. Longmans Green, 1894.

Holmes, A., *Principles of Physical Geology*. Nelson, 1965.

King, L. C., *Morphology of the Earth*. Oliver and Boyd, 1962.

Leaky, L. S. B., *Olduvai Gorge, 1951-61*. Cambridge University Press, 1965.

Luther, E. W., *Ethiopia Today*. Oxford University Press, 1958.

Mackworth-Praed, C. W. and Grant, C. H. B., *Birds of Eastern and Northeastern Africa (2 Vols.)*. International Publications Service, 1960.

Marcus, H. G., *The Modern History of Ethiopia and the Horn of Africa: A Select and Annotated Bibliography*. Hoover Institute, 1971.

Mohr, P. A., *The Geology of Ethiopia*. University College of Addis Ababa Press, 1964.

Moorehead, A., *No Room in the Ark*. Hamish Hamilton, 1959.

Morgan, W. T. W., (ed.), *East Africa: Its Peoples and Resources*. London University Press, 1969.

Morgan, W. T. W., *East Africa*. Longman, 1973.

Nesbitt, L. M., *Desert and Forest*. Jonathan Cape, 1934, Penguin, 1955.

Richards, C. G., *Count Teleki and the Discovery of Lakes Rudolf and Stefanie*. Macmillan, 1960.

Tazieff, H., *South from the Red Sea*. Lutterworth Press, 1956.

Thomson, J., *Through Masai Land*. Low, Marston, Searle & Rivington, 1885.

Williams, J. G., *A Field Guide to the Birds of East and Central Africa*. Collins, 1963.

Williams, J. G., *A Field Guide to the National Parks of East Africa*. Collins, 1967.

Younghusband, E., *Glimpses of East Africa and Zanzibar*. John Long, 1910.

Acknowledgements

The author and editors of this book wish to thank the following: Anglia Television, London; Dr. William Bishop, London; Suzie Bower, London; Christopher Chant, London; Members of Staff of the Foreign Office Library, London; Dan Freeman, London; Derek T. Harris, Los Angeles; Imperial Chemical Industries, London; The Magadi Soda Company, Northwich, Cheshire; Alan and Joan Root, Kenya; Members of Staff of the Royal Geographical Society Library, London; Donald Simpson, Librarian, Royal Commonwealth Society, London; Dr. Emil Urban, Addis Ababa; Dr. G. E. Wickens, Royal Botanical Gardens, London; Members of Staff of the Library of the Zoological Society, London.

Picture Credits

Sources for pictures in this book are shown below. Credits for pictures from left to right are separated by commas.

All photographs are by Goetz D. Plage, from Bruce Coleman Ltd., London, except: Cover–Lee Lyon from Bruce Coleman Ltd. Front end papers 1, 2–M. R. Stanley Price from Natural Science Photos, London. Front end paper 3, page 1–Klaus Paysan. 4, 5–Lee Lyon. 8, 9–A. J. Dean from Bruce Coleman Ltd. 14, 15–Map by Hunting Surveys Ltd., London. 19–National Aeronautics and Space Administration. 23–M. R. Stanley Price from Natural Science Photos. 24–Royal Geographical Society, London. 29–Dr. Ian Gibson from Robert Harding Associates, London. 30 to 33–Gerald Cubitt. 34, 35–Dr. Georg Gerster from the John Hillelson Agency, London. 36, 37–Gerald Cubitt. 41–Lee Lyon. 45–Lee Lyon. 49 to 59–Dr. Georg Gerster from the John Hillelson Agency. 71–Norman Myers from Bruce Colman Ltd. 82–Map by Hunting Surveys Ltd. 94–Colin Willock. 101–Jane Burton from Bruce Coleman Ltd. 107–A. J. Sutcliffe from Natural Science Photos. 108, 109–Lee Lyon. 110–Leslie Brown from Ardea Photographics, London. 111–Lee Lyon. 112, 113–W. B. Bishop. 114, 115–Douglas Botting. 118–Peter Hill. 123–John Moss from Colorific Photo Library Ltd., London. 124–Leslie Brown from Ardea Photographics. 125–Jane Burton from Bruce Coleman Ltd. 127–Douglas Botting. 128–Mark Boulton. 129–Douglas Botting. 130, 131–C. Weaver from Ardea Photographics. 136, 137–Mirella Ricciardi, *Vanishing Africa*, Collins, London. 142–Map by Hunting Surveys Ltd. 143 to 151–from *Discovery by Count Teleki of Lakes Rudolf and Stefanie* by his companion Lieut. Ludwig von Höhnel, 1894. 160–Iain and Oria Douglas-Hamilton. 162, 163–Iain and Oria Douglas-Hamilton. 169–John Dominis. 170, 171–Horst Munzig from Susan Griggs, London. 172, 173–Lee Lyon. 174, 175–Teleki-Baldwin. 177–John Dominis. 178, 179–Jane Burton from Bruce Coleman Ltd.

Index

*Numerals in italics indicate a
photograph or drawing of the subject
mentioned.*

A

Abbe, lake, 44
Abhebad, lake, 42-43
Abiata, lake, 60, 61, 66, 67
Abili Agituk, volcano, *112-113*
Acacia trees, 64, 76, 84, 90, 97, 103, 153,
   154, 156
Adabada, lake, 42
Adjutant storks, *see* Storks, marabou
Afar triangle, *see* Danakil desert
Afar tribe, 27, 38, 39, 42, 46, 47; tribal
   hut, *41*
Algae, *4-5*, 40, *110*, *112-113*, 117
Alkaline lakes, *see* Soda lakes
Ants, 84
Augur buzzards, 88, *88*
Aussa, Sultanate of, 42, 43
Australopithecus boisei, 134
Awash, river, 38, 40-43, *45*, 60

B

Baboons, 91, *91*, 97, 154, *157*
Bananas, 158, 166
Baobab trees, 153-154
Baringo basin, 22, 24
Baringo, lake, 18; crocodile population,
   69, 72; fauna, 60; geology, 22, 24;
   reason for fresh water, 73
Basalt, 97
Basso Narok, 20; *see also* Rudolf, lake
Bee-eaters, white-fronted, 92-93, *93*
Beetles, dung-, 93-94
Bird life, 26, 43, 68, 69, 76, 99
Brown, Leslie, 61, 62, 64, 69, 103-105, 119
Buck apples, *see* Sodom apples
Buffalo, *144*
Bume tribe, 135-136
Butterflies, 91-92, *92*

C

Calderas, 36, 94
Canthaxanthin, 122
Cheesman, Major Robert, 46
Circumcision, 147

Continental drift, 20, 25
Cormorants, *130-131*
Cranes, *148*
Craters, volcanic, 34, *34*, *35*, 36, *36*, *37*,
   94; *see also* Calderas
Crickets, mole, *101*
Crocodiles, 43, 60, 70, *71*, 150;
   aggressiveness, 72; breeding grounds,
   69; distribution, 69; in lake Jipe, 144
Cubitt, Gerald, 28, 30

D

Dallol, Mount, 46, 48, *50-57*
Danakil Depression, 38; *see also*
   Danakil desert
Danakil desert, *19*, 27, 28, 38, *45*;
   earthquakes, 39; explorers, 40-43;
   geological history, 39, 40; salt plains,
   39
Danakil tribe, *see* Afar tribe
Dassies, 88-89
Denhardt, Clemens, 18
Desenech tribe, 135
Diatoms, 117
Dik-diks, 85, *157*
Dissotis flowers, 94, *94*
Douglas-Hamilton, Dr. Iain, 156,
   158-159, 160, 164-166, 167
Dragonflies, *101*
Ducks, shoveler, 120
Duikers, 84

E

Eagles: fish, *74*, *75*, 76, *78-79*; martial,
   85; Verreaux's, 88
Earthquakes, 39
Earwigs, *101*
Egrets, cattle, 43, 80
Elands, 91, 148, 168, *177*
Electric fences, 166
Elephants, 27, 149-150, *149*; adolescent
   bulls, 160-161, *163*; communication,
   160; ecological problems, 158,
   166-167; family units, 160-161, *162*,
   163, 164-166; feeding, 158, *160*; group
   movements, 164-167; protection of
   herd members, *163*, 164;
   radio-tracking, 164-166; studies of
   social behaviour, 158-159, 164-166
Elgeyo scarp, 22, 24
El Molo tribe, 136, 140-141

Embarta, 90, *90*
Endabash, 167
Erta-ale, volcano, 28, 34, *34*
Eruptions, volcanic, 15, 21, 25; effusive,
   28, 34; explosive, 28, 34
Ethiopia, 38, 46, 60

F

Fever trees, 84, *84*
Fig trees, 153
Fischer, Dr. Gustav, 18, 88
Fischer's Column, 88, *89*
Fish, 60-61; black bass, 76; catfish, 43;
   Nile perch, 70, 72; tilapia, 67, 69, 76,
   99-100, 120
Fishing, 137-138, *138-139*, 140-141
Flamingoes, *end papers 3-page 1*, 26, 60,
   96, 106, *110*, *123*, *130-131*; breeding,
   119, *119*; colouration, 122;
   courtship display, 118-119;
   distribution, 117; feeding, 117, 118,
   122; flight, 116-117; greater, 117, 122,
   124, *125*; lesser, 117, 122, *126*, *127*, *128*,
   129; nesting grounds, 103; predators,
   122; specialized bill, 118, 122
Formic acid, 84
"1470 man", 134
Freshwater lakes, 60, 73-76
Fumaroles, *see* Hot springs

G

Galla tribes, 61, 136
Gamarri, lake, 43
Gazelles, *157*; *see also* Soemmering's
   gazelles; Thomson's gazelles
Gerenuks, *145*, 168, *169*
Gill-netting, 137, *138-139*
Giraffes, 94, 168, *170*
Gondwanaland, 20, 25
Gnus, 168; *see also* Wildebeeste
Graben, 20, 21
Grasshoppers, wingless, 88, *88*
Great Rift Valley: age, 17, 25, 26; before
   subsidence, 22; early explorations,
   18-25; first maps, 18; formation, 24,
   25-26; geological section, 21, 22-24;
   legends about formation, 17-18;
   length, 17; photograph taken from
   Apollo spacecraft, 18, *19*; rainfall, 46,

78, 106; tribes, 27, 132, 134-141;
  wildlife, 26, 27, 76, 168; see also
  Bird life, Fish, Plants, Trees
Gregory, John Walter, 20-25, 24, 73, 96
Gregory Rift, 25
Guano, 64
Gypsum, 57

H

Hell's Gate, 82, 82-94, 89, 95
Herons: goliath, 2-3, 80; squacco, 80
Hillaby, Dr. John, 140
Hippopotamus, 43, 82-83, 144, 168,
  172-173
Höhnel, Ludwig von, 20, 142
Homo sapiens, 134
Hopcroft, John, 117
Hot springs, 39, 47, 48, 50-51, 54-55, 99,
  102-103
Hummingbirds, 148

I

Impala, 91, 155
Indian Ocean, formation of, 25-26

J

Jacana, see Lily-trotters
Jackals, 86, 168, 174-175
Jipe, lake, 144
Jira, Mount, 42, 43

K

Kamasia, 22, 24, 25
Kapedo, 73
Karum salt lake, 44-47, 48, 49, 50-51,
  58-59
Kenya Fisheries Department, 137
Kenya, Mount, 148
Kerio, river, 22
Kikuyuland, 147
Kikuyu scarp, 96
Kikuyu tribe, 27, 147-148
Kilimanjaro, Mount, 144, 147; see also
  Szek, Count Samuel Teleki
Kinangop plateau, 76
Kingfishers, malachite, 77, 79; pied,
  79-80; woodland, 79
Kinship groups, 160
Koobi Fora, 134

L

Laikipia escarpment, 22, 24
Lammergeiers, 89, 89
Lava lakes, 28, 34
Leakey, Richard, 133-134, 141
Lengai, Mount, cover, 18, 30, 32, 33, 100,
  102; alkalinity, 106; volcanic
  activity, 28, 29, 30-31
Leonotis, 87, 87
Leopards, 142, 143, 144, 148, 157
Lily-trotters, 80-81
Lions, 6-7, 154, 168, 178-179
Loiengalani, 140, 141
Longonot, volcano, 36, 37, 82, 83, 95;
  geological age, 94; volcanic ash,
  89-90
Lorian island, 140

M

Magadi, lake, 76, 96, 97-100, 106, 107
Magma, 28
Mahogany trees, 153
Manyara: elephants, 152-157; trees,
  153-156; vegetation, 153; water, 153,
  167; wildlife, 153, 154
Manyara escarpment, 152-153
Manyara, lake, 18, 152
Manyara National Park, 152
Marang Forest Reserve, 166
Marmots, 148
Masailand, 18, 21-22, 146, 147
Masai tribe, 27, 97, 132, 146
Menengai, volcano, 36
Mohr, Paul, 34
Monkeys, Blue Sykes, 154
Mto-wa-Mbu, 158, 166
Murchison Falls Park, 158
Mursi tribe, 135-136

N

Nabuyatom, volcano, 112-113
Naivasha, lake, 21, 27, 82, 98; bird life,
  76, 79-81; fauna, 60; rainfall, 78;
  reason for fresh water, 76;
  vegetation, 76
Nakuru, lake, 116, 117-118; wildlife,
  120-121
Nakuru National Park, 117
Natron, lake, end papers 1-2, 96,
  103-105, 106, 108-109, 110, 111;
  visual deception, 100-102

Nature, balance of, 168
Nesbitt, L. M., 40, 42
Ngong Hills, 97
Ngongo Bagas, 147
Nilotic tribes, 132, 135
Njemps tribe, 27, 73
Nyanza swifts, 87-88
Nyika, 144

O

Obsidian, 44, 92, 92
Ol Doinyo Lengai, see Lengai, Mount
Olduvai Gorge, 134
Omo, river, 69, 72, 106, 114-115; delta,
  134-135; see also Crocodiles
Ornaments, tribal, 146-147, 147
Oryx, 102
Ostriches, 44, 85, 85, 102

P

Papyrus, 76, 79-80
Pastori, T., 40
Pelican Island, 62-64
Pelicans, great white, 43, 61, 63, 65;
  breeding grounds, 62, 64; courtship
  displays, 64; feeding habits, 64, 66,
  66, 67; fishing grounds, 69; on lake
  Nakuru, 120
Plants, succulent, 91
Poisoned arrows, 147

R

Radio-tracking, 164-166
Rain forests, 27, 144-145
Reedbucks, 84
Rendille tribe, 136
Reichenow's weavers, 86
Reshiat tribe, 150
Rhinoceroses, 154
Rift, definition of, 24
Rock hyrax, see Dassies
Root, Alan, 100, 119, 153
Rosina, G., 40
Rudolf, lake, 8-9; algae, 112-113;
  alkalinity, 60-61; bird life, 106;
  crocodile population, 69, 70;
  discovery, 20, 142, 148-149; fish life,
  106; in prehistoric times, 133, 141;
  prehistoric wildlife, 133; tribes, 132,
  134-141

S
Salt, 46, *58-59*
Salt lakes, 44-47, 48, *49*, *58-59*
Sandgrouse, chestnut-bellied, 68
Savannah, 84, 154
Secretary birds, 86, *86*, 87
Sedges, *see* Papyrus
Senecio johnstonii, 148, *148*
Shala, lake, 60-67
Shifta, the, 136
Shrikes, fiscal, 87
Snakes, 86, 87
Soda flats, 99-100, 102, 103-105, *107*
Soda lakes, 26, 96-106, *108-109*
Soda springs, *4-5*
Soda, washing, 26, 96, 98, 106
Sodium carbonate, *see* Soda, washing
Sodium chloride, *see* Salt
Sodom apples, 91, *91*
Solanum bushes, 91
Somalis, 17
Sonjo tribe, 153
Star grass, *84*
Stefanie, lake, 20, 142, 150
Stinkbark, 153
Storks, 97, *146*; marabou, 120-121
Suess, Eduard, 20

Suguta Valley, 140, 141
Sunbirds, 87
Suswa, volcano, 36
Swamps, 43
Szek, Count Samuel Teleki von, *see*
    Teleki, Count Samuel

T
Taveta, 144-147, *146*, *147*
Teleki, Count Samuel, 20, 132, 140, *144*;
    discovery of lakes Rudolf and
    Stefanie, 142, 148-149, 150; 1887
    expedition into the interior, 142, *142*,
    143-150, *151*
Telemetry, 164
Tessema, Ato Berhane, 61
Thermal columns, 66, 67
Thermal springs, *see* Hot springs
Thesiger, Wilfred, 40-43
Thomson, Joseph, 18
Thomson's gazelles, 87, *87*, 97, 99
Thorn trees, 84, 85
Tilapia fish, 67, 69, 76
Tilapia grahami, 99-100, 120
Tugen Hills, *see* Kamasia
Turkana tribe, 136-140, *138-139*

U
Uaso Nyiro, river, 102
Urban, Dr. Emil, 61, 62, 64, 69

V
Volcanic activity, 25, 26, 28, *29-37*, 39
Volcanoes, 28, 47; *see also* Erta-ale,
    Gelai, Jira, Lengai, Longonot,
    Menengai, Shombole, Silali, Suswa
Vultures, bearded, 146; *see also*
    Lammergeiers

W
Wagtails, African pied, 80
Wakefield, T., 18
Wakwafi tribe, 146
Waterbucks, 148, 168, *176*
Water cress, 153
Water lilies, 76, 80-81
Weaver birds, 86, *86*, 97
Wildebeeste, 102; *see also* Gnus
Wildlife, threat to, 168

Z
Zebras, 85, 99, 102, 148

XXXX

Colour reproduction by
Printing Developments International Ltd.,
Leeds, England—a Time Inc. subsidiary.
Filmsetting by C. E. Dawkins (Typesetters) Ltd., London, SE1 1UN.
Printed in Holland by Smeets Lithographers, Weert.
Bound by Proost en Brandt N.V., Amsterdam.